# "...BUT WHERE ARE YOU REALLY FROM?"

# "...BUT WHERE ARE YOU REALLY FROM?"

Anthologised and Edited
by
HAZELLE PALMER

Sister Vision
Black Women and Women of Colour Press

97 98 99 00 01 02 ML 6 5 4 3 2 1

Canadian Cataloguing in Publication Data

...but where are you really from

ISBN 0-896705-20-0

I. Canadian literature (English) - Minority authors.* 2. Canadian literature (English) – Women authors.* 3. Canadian literature (English) – 20th century.* 4. Minority women – Canada – Literary collections. 5. Ethnicity – Canada – Literary collections. 6. Racism – Canada – Literary collections. 7. Canada – Race relations – Literary collections. 8. Assimilation (Sociology) – Literary collections.
I. Palmer, Hazelle.
PS8235.W7B87 1997     C810.8'0355     C97-931004-0
PR9194.5W6B87 1997

Cover Art: © Hazelle Palmer
Book Design: michéle
Editor for the Press: Makeda Silvera

*Sister Vision Press acknowledges the financial support of the Canada Council and the Ontario Arts Council towards its publishing program.*

*The editor gratefully acknowledges the financial support of the Multiculturalism and Heritage Branch of the Department of the Secretary of State.*

Represented in Canada by the Literary Press Group
Distributed in Canada by General Distribution Services
Represented and distributed in the U.S.A. by Login/InBook
Represented in Britain by Turnaround Distribution

Printed in Canada by union labour

SISTER VISION
Black Women and Women of Colour Press
P.O. Box 217, Station E
Toronto, Ontario
Canada  M6H 4E2
(416) 533-9353

FOR ASHAE

# INTRODUCTION

identity n. The fact of being the same in all
respects; who a person is, or what a thing is;
a statement of equality which is true under
all conditions.

*Webster's Encyclopedic Dictionary*
*(Canadian edition)*

IN this the age of identity politics, "...BUT WHERE ARE YOU *REALLY FROM?*" couldn't be more timely. In it women of colour discuss what identity is, where it comes from and how to claim it. Mixed into these writings are thoughts about assimilation and its importance and about what immigrants lose in making cultural adjustments.

A sense of belonging in Canada is elusive for those of us who share part of our lives here. No matter how long we or our families have lived here, we are still not readily accepted as Canadian. It is frustrating to be born or raised in a country where you are constantly made to feel like an outsider.

## What Does a Canadian Look Like?

Where are you *really* from? or Where are your parents from? are loaded questions for people of colour born or raised in Canada. The questions suggest that we do not "look" Canadian. It also suggests that the questioner, perhaps unknowingly, needs to match us to a country that he or she thinks is more representative of what we *do* look like: if we are Black, it probably means Jamaica; if we are Asian, it means China or Hong Kong. This probing of our ancestry keeps us forever foreign, forever immigrants to Canada. Moreover, the questions are by nature racist; their faulty premise assumes that because we are not White we could not be Canadian. Their logic is based on colonialist and racist assumptions about what Canadians look like and what it is to be Canadian.

## Origins

My reasons for preparing this anthology are simple: I was tired of explaining my background to satisfy some unwanted curiosity about me, tired of being told that I am not Canadian because I do not "look" Canadian, tired of having to explain why I am Canadian. I have pondered the meaning of identity for years, wondering what it is, where it comes from, and how non-White children who are raised in predominantly White societies fit into a culture that largely counts them out. Over the past few years, I have been talking to others about growing up Black in Canada, about how I balance Canadian culture with my ancestral culture, about why my survival and self-esteem demand I hold on to both and about how, despite my efforts, I still feel isolated from both cultures at times. Those conversations were cathartic for everyone: it was as though we had needed to say out loud what we had been thinking all our lives; we had an informal forum to talk passionately about why identity keeps people rooted, gives people a sense of themselves in the world, about why we had yet to feel that for ourselves.

We discussed when immigrants should become fully integrated or assimilated into a new society. We wondered whether identity should be as malleable as clay, to be moulded many ways. Those conversations were the catalyst I needed to put my thoughts on paper. I wanted to move beyond conversations with friends and find out whether the issues we talked about were of consequence to others.

They are. Joining me in this anthology are thirty-two women and one man. Like me, they are hyphenated Canadians: Black-Canadians, South Asian-Canadians, Filipino-Canadians, Native-Canadians, Chinese-Canadians, Japanese-Canadians ... The hyphenation is a compromise: it relieves mainstream White society of its responsibility for accepting us as just Canadians and it makes us feel secure to know that another culture helps us define who we are. We would not argue against throwing out the hyphens once and for all, for just being seen as ourselves and not our ethnic origins. As our stories illustrate, racism prevents us from ever doing this.

The writers share the anger, humour, frustration and isolation they have faced in trying to fit in and the resolutions they have come to. Some of the stories have similar themes: childhood memories that both hurt and strengthened, threats to self-esteem, a sense of vulnerability while growing up, eruptions of anger when asked where they come from, shame at recognizing how uncomfortable they feel being around others from their ethnic group or while wearing ethnic dress, surprise at resolving that identity is really a combination of all that gives them roots, all that ultimately creates a new "Canadian" identity.

Others, such as a mixed-race, lesbian, Jamaican-born woman who has lived in Canada for more than twenty-five years and who has finally found what identity and community mean to her, bring unique perspectives.

The submissions came from Nova Scotia, The Northwest Territories, Alberta, Ontario, Quebec and British Columbia. The voices are genuine. There is no lengthy academic analysis here. I wanted to know that anyone could read and appreciate what we are saying and be stronger and more aware for having done so.

The writers are non-White. Throughout the two years I spent calling for submissions, I heard from a number of women from Eastern European, Russian, Portuguese and Italian backgrounds and I heard from Jewish women. Each had experiences that were similar to those discussed here, but theirs focused largely on how to establish one's identity if one was born or raised in one environment while one's parents were born or raised in another. I heard and read stories where language and stricter norms and traditions created serious conflicts within families and within communities. How we learn to balance two worlds is discussed here, but the White women's stories are not included. It was important for me to hear from women of colour. I strongly believe that while women of Russian and European descent and Jewish women can draw some parallels between their experiences and those of non-White women, there is still considerable distance between them. Our colour makes us visible and this visibility contributes to people making assumptions about our identity. It is difficult for me to imagine that it is the same for Eastern European or other White women or that these women will ever know what it is like to be discriminated against because of race, for they are visibly part of the mainstream, part of the White majority. For Jewish women, anti-Semitism is as painful as racism is for women of colour, but, for me, anti-Semitism — and the culture clashes other White women are dealing with — belongs in another anthology. Extending the discussion to include those issues would distract from the point of this anthology: that systemic racism in all its many guises ensures that no matter how long non-White Canadians are here we will always be treated differently. No matter how much we assimilate, we will never be accepted as being Canadian. We will always be asked where we are *really* from.

This anthology is divided into six sections. The first, **Where Are You Really From?**, tackles head-on the question that prompted it, a question that provokes anger, pain and frustration. Humour, down-and-out vents, poetry and biographical essays strip the question bare to reveal its underlying assumption: you can't be from here because you don't look "Canadian."

But we are here, we are Canadian. The second section, **Fitting In**, explores assimilation: how easy or difficult it is, what issues arise, how race and class fit in. The challenge is not always from mainstream society. Even our own ethnic or racial communities can make us feel awkward. Nadine Leggett, in "Struggle for Identity: Seven Black Canadian Women Share Their Experiences," quotes one woman as saying, "I was fifteen before I was actually in a room of Black people and I was very uncomfortable."

"Every time the teacher mentioned 'black,' 'ape' or 'Africa' she looked at me," remembers one woman. Such statements characterise what it is like to grow up in a predominately-White environment where, in most cases, the images society reinforces in school and in the larger community perpetuate racist stereotypes about Black people. Indeed, the actions of one person can leave an indelible imprint on our lives.

The third section, **Mirror, Mirror**, takes a look at how we see ourselves and how others see us. Do we see ourselves as attractive or beautiful? If not, whose standards are we using to judge? Why is important to us to feel as though our unique beauty is appreciated? Are we Black or Brown or women of colour? How have labels become political triggers? Such questions point to the need for us to see ourselves represented as we are and to be appreciated, not isolated, for our differences. In "Soul Sounds" Carol Talbot says:

> We are children of disinheritance
>   lost on a sea of illusions
> Mirrors reflect not ourselves
>   only shadows of selves past
>   and distorted images of their present

How we imagine ourselves in Canada is always linked to our past. But our environment also affects how feel about ourselves now and is directly connected to our self-esteem. Somewhere along the line of our ancestral ties and where we are now, we have to force ourselves to see who we truly are. We may be far removed from where our ancestors started out, but it is what we have to live with. In coming to terms with this, we can forget about how society sees us or defines us and learn to define ourselves for ourselves.

Section four, **Isolation**, looks at what it is like to live in an environment that is unaccepting, an environment where race, language and culture create barriers that keep you separate. Lisa Valencia-Svensson writes:

> The fragmentation
>     is so overpowering.
> I am alone in a white world
> And the barriers
>     that divide me
>     from other women of colour
>     are immense.

Cultural identity binds people together on many levels. In its absence we are naturally drawn to others whose interests and struggles are similar to our own. It is an instinctive part of survival. But when language, race, ethnicity and nationality keep us from supporting each other, even that pull can weaken.

**Language and Identity** is the focus of section five. Ayanna Black writes about her apprehension about writing in Jamaican Creole. Her feeling may be familiar to those who recall that the Creoles, once considered to be non-standard English, were discouraged. It is only fairly recently that we have begun to see, through dub poetry and other forms, the revitalisation of native Caribbean languages. However, whether the Creoles are truly accepted within North American literary circles or in the broader culture or whether colonialist notions that these languages are "bad English" or evidence of "poor class" or "poor education" will prevail is still open to question. Camille Hernandez-Ramdwar's essay, "The Creation of Identity: Challenges for Women of Colour Writers," notes:

> The struggle to create or to maintain an identity has been a complex one for women of colour living in the West. Much of our work, our creativity, is fraught with it. On the frontier of the written word, voice, appropriation, colonial language and access have been at the forefront. We can only write from our own perspectives.

No discussion of language, identity and assimilation would be complete without mention of the loss we feel when the pressure of assimilation makes us lose our mother tongues. How can we measure that loss? What is its impact? Particularly for young children, it can mean losing an aspect of culture that would help them in the years to come, help them feel connected, not isolated. We know it isn't enough to speak English to be accepted here. Immigrants have always had to depend on their own communities for the support they couldn't find in the broader "Canadian" society, but where do young people who have lost their native languages turn? Susan Lee's poem "Mother Tongue" captures the loss:

> My mother tongue
> swallowed, digested and
> expelled
> almost forgotten except
> for the taste which lingers in my mouth.

The final section, **Finding "Home,"** tells how the contributors define themselves, their communities and, ultimately, their homes. Most have reached peace of mind, although, in some cases, the journey continues. The writers have taken their experiences and moulded them into a new creation. They have found "home," and the realisation is worthy of rejoicing.

## Resolution

This anthology is itself a journey. It begins with the need for acceptance, moves on to what makes it elusive, then to gradual clarity and, finally, straight through to finding "home." Not everyone featured here has completed the journey, and some may still find it too far to reach, but that the writers have put their thoughts on paper, have spoken of it sometimes for the first time, is a step forward in accepting ourselves for who we are and an invitation to others to do the same.

I would like to thank all the contributors to this anthology. Their experiences, thoughts and ideas have enriched my journey as I determine my identity and find my place within Canadian society. I hope they, in turn, will find this anthology a tangible expression of their innermost feelings and that it gives them faith in the future.

This book is dedicated to my daughter Ashae. I hope that she, a second-generation Canadian, will find a better sense of herself and of belonging here than I have found. But if she doesn't, I trust she will read the stories in this anthology, feel encouraged by them and know that she is not alone.

Hazelle Palmer ~ 1997

# TABLE OF CONTENTS

# ONE

# Where Are You Really From?

**Althea Samuels**

# Identity: How Do I Define Mine

SHE comes racing at me from across the room, a bundle of mis-spent energy, all wired-up and wide-eyed. She bounces into my face like a firecracker about to explode.

"Hello! Hi, I'm sorry I just had to come over and talk to you. I just need to know: Where are you from?"

"Umm ... I'm ..." I'm thinking to myself, Does she really want to know where I'm from? Do I tell her I was born here? Do I tell her my parents are Jamaican? Do I tell her I'm Jamaican? Do I tell her I don't know what she means? Do I tell her I think that's an odd question to be asking someone at an anti-racism rally?

She's still looking at me, her face glowing with expectancy, waiting for some exotic story of my origins.

"She's Canadian. She was born here," my friend pipes in.

Friend is conveniently ignored.

"I'm from here," I say.

"Oh, but I mean originally."

"She was born here." Friend's voice is rising.

"My parents are from Jamaica."

"Oh Jamaica, isn't that nice."

"But she's Canadian."

"I come to these events all the time. I think they're very important. I think they're needed."

I nod in agreement, in amazement, in disbelief.

It's not that I don't get asked that a lot. It happens almost daily but never in that kind of setting. We had just finished attending workshops, videos and a theatre presentation about racism and prejudice. For a woman who had just been through all of that to come up to me and basically say, "You're Black, you can't be from here" was just too much.

It's probably the clearest indication I've had that you can have all the anti-racism forums, discussions, whatever, but you can't change what's been ingrained into the hearts and minds of people.

Canada is the land of my birth and the closest place to what I could call home. Yet I don't call it home. I don't call Canada my home because I know I'm not accepted here. Home is somewhere where you know you're loved, where you're accepted for who you are, and because of that acceptance and love, you are inspired with the confidence and courage to grow and to become who you want to be. I don't see or feel that here.

I used to believe that I would never amount to anything. I had three strikes against me, I thought. I was Black, a woman and disabled (I have a form of palsy that has left my right arm partially paralysed).

But I was wrong. As I learned more and more about my history, I learned just how powerful and important the Africans and, in particular, African women are. I learned that disability does not mean inability. I learned about the great civilisations of Africa and the people who ruled them. I learned about slavery, not from a guilt-saving, European point-of-view, but from a human one and could see it for what it really was. No longer did I feel shame that my ancestors were slaves because I realised the shame was not mine or any other African's to bear.

I learned how Africans united, against heavy odds, and rose above the inhumanity of slavery. I learned about Queen Nzingha and Harriet Tubman, just two of the many powerful and awe-inspiring women in African history.

I learned about the involvement and leadership of Africans in medicine, chemistry and inventions worldwide.

What a shame to be learning at twenty what would have been a definite boost to my self-esteem as a child.

Teachers were another story. I had one who, after I handed in an assignment, held it up as an example of the way things were done in my culture. He then went into some explanation about matriarchal and patriarchal societies and said that where I am from the woman is considered in control and more important than the man.

The assignment had been to draw our family tree. I put my mother's family on the right-hand side and my father's on the left. Everyone else did the opposite. The truth was I didn't realise there was a formula we were supposed to be following. My teacher's "insight" and his instruction on "my culture" were quite the eye-openers for me.

That same teacher came up to me on the playground one cold winter day and asked me why I looked so much warmer than everyone else. He said he found that very interesting and that it was something someone should look into one day. Then he smiled and walked away.

Then there was the teacher at college who told me that he didn't think it was a very good idea to put Caribbean music in my video production because of its association with AIDS ... What?

"Where are you from?"

Now when I'm asked that question the answer I give is: "Jamaica. Well, my parents are from Jamaica. I was born here." Many Jamaicans have told me I was born in Canada, that I should call myself Canadian. But, at the same time, if I say I'm Canadian I'm greeted with nasty looks that say "Who do you think you are? Are you trying to deny your heritage?"

Identity. How do I define mine? That's the key. I define *mine*.

I see myself as an African. That's the land of my ancestors, that's where I would be if it wasn't for the holocaust they call the slave trade, but I know that many Africans would not see me as African and would not like my identifying myself that way.

My maternal grandfather was born in Africa, but it's not known where. He worked and travelled with Marcus Garvey and was killed in prison because of his beliefs. When he was murdered, a large chunk of our history died with him.

At times, I feel empty and lost, like I'm in an abyss, caught in the middle of nowhere, not accepted anywhere. I find solace in knowing this earth is not my final resting place. I am on a journey, just passing through.

So the next time anyone asks me where I'm from, I'll tell them, "The question is where am I going? Where I'm from was stolen from me long ago."

**Mutriba Din**

# Where Are You From?

**WHERE** Are You From?
(Oh, shit. Not again.)
Polite smile: I was born in Kenya, moved to London, England, when I was ten, and then to Regina when I was twelve, and to Calgary when I was seventeen. My parents were born in Kenya. My grandparents were born in India/Pakistan. I am a Punjabi Muslim.

(Damn! Why did I tell my life story?)

~~~

Once I tried this answer:

"Calgary."

(I try and say it seriously, without shrugging my shoulders, trying to be nonchalant, without smiling awkwardly.)

NO, NO, NO ... WHERE ARE YOU REALLY FROM? (ARE YOU TRYING TO BE FUNNY?)

Polite smile: "I was born in Kenya, moved ..."

~~~

Another time, I said I never wanted to hear the question again.

BUT IT'S NOT A RACIST QUESTION. I ALWAYS ASK PEOPLE WHERE THEY'RE FROM. I'M CURIOUS ABOUT PEOPLE. I GET ASKED ALL THE TIME BECAUSE OF MY SCOTTISH ACCENT AND I DON'T MIND BEING ASKED. DON'T BE SO SENSITIVE.

(Why don't I, why can't I, respond with a brilliantly cutting answer and make people realise what they are asking?)

Because racism catches me unaware, shocks me, silences me, I politely smile, politely answer.

### Hazelle Palmer

# Living in Two Worlds

**I'M** on my way to Cuba. A little R & R. Catch up on some reading. Try to put my life back in order. But I'm already feeling pressure because I have only seven days to do all that. No matter... I've earned this trip. It's been a long and arduous year. Hard work and insufficient time left over to fit in the rest of my life. But this will be good. Sandy beaches, warm water, hot sun. The sun is what I crave most: to wrap myself completely in the sun's steaming heat — no sun protection (I'll pay for that later). I'm just so cold, it seems it will take forever for me to warm up.

It's time to board the plane. I'm excited, and though there is much to think about and examine, I'm sure this trip will revitalise me. I'm on my own for seven glorious, sun-baking, rum-drinking, fruit-slurping, decadent days. I make my way down the narrow aisle of Royal Airlines. The plane is overstuffed with pale people all looking forward to the getaway. Half way to my seat, I overhear one woman tell her travelling companion, "Oh! Look, honey, there's a Cuban girl on the plane!"

Oh, shit. It's gonna be one of those trips. I find my seat and stare out the window at the frozen ground.

~~~

I was born in London, England. My parents met there in the fifties after emigrating from their separate islands — Barbados and Jamaica. I can't remember much about England. Of what I do remember, I'm uncertain where my memories end and the years of watching too many British television programs begin. I remember a lot of concrete, grey buildings and weather to match. I remember the children at school asking me why the palms of my hands weren't black like the other sides and if the bottoms of my feet were the same. I remember being called "Sambo" and "monkey."

I remember we lived in a house with a bright yellow door with a huge number five bolted to it. I remember that my father taught me how to ride my first bicycle, a red and white number that stunned the other children on the block and made me feel especially proud.

7

In 1966, when I was seven years old, my family immigrated to Canada. We settled in Montreal in a small community called The Gardens. There you could find people from all races, but they were all working-class or new immigrants. For the latter, The Gardens represented a first step, one of many that would take them on their "upward" journey in Canada. The rent was reasonable, and it was centrally located. It was a good spot to catch yourself when you just arrived, so you could save a little, so you could move on.

My family lived in The Gardens for about five years. During that time, my sister and I experienced racism that was different from what we had known in Britain. Canadians seemed to be more subtle about it. We didn't call it systemic racism then, we were just children. We didn't even call it racism. We just knew that we were treated differently, and it was confusing because at times it was mixed with classism.

At the school we attended, the classes were divided into three groups: advanced, average and remedial. All the children from The Gardens were in the remedial group. Now that was fine at first. After all, they were our first friends, the children we hopped the fence with every day to go to school, the ones we'd play with each evening and on weekends, so sitting together in class was an extension of our play-time. But I began to notice that I wasn't learning very much. My report cards bore this out, and the more I paid attention, the less attention I was paid.

My sister and I talked it over, but it was difficult to explain our frustrations to our parents. Like so many others, I'm sure, they believed whole-heartedly that we only had to show up at school, pay attention, and anything would be possible.

I was told once that if White kids were performing one-hundred percent, Black kids had to perform two-hundred percent to succeed. My sister and I found this to be true. Throughout our grade-school years, on into high school and university, it wasn't enough to do our best. We had to out-perform: read more than the assigned chapters, do the best class projects, deliver the best presentations and write essays worthy of publication, and even then, A marks proved very elusive.

I remember approaching a high-school guidance counsellor for advice. I was finishing up my college/CEGEP entrance application. He told me flatly that the best I could aim for was to be a domestic worker. My marks were better than average, I was a good student, and I had my sights set on being a lawyer. I was stunned by what he said. While I ignored him and successfully filled in the application on my own, I've often wondered how many other Black children received that advice, wondered how many dreams were crushed by his ignorance and racism.

As with so many other non-White people, my life in Canada has included many of those encounters. For me, identity has never been about fitting into White middle-class Canadian society but about being accepted as being a Canadian who happens to be Black. It is an acknowledgement that is extended without hesitation to the children of White immigrants, to people who, like me, are also first-generation Canadians. For them, becoming assimilated is a far different journey. The constant questioning of where I am from perpetually undermines my sense of belonging. For me, finding my identity has been a battle; it has been so because Black people and others from visible minority groups are not readily accepted here. Even multi-culturalism, which professes to maintain and celebrate the myriad of cultures in Canada, continues to regard people of colour as the Other. It does not allow us to contribute to a redefinition of Canadianness. Instead, it helps maintain the status quo work and keeps us on the outside.

When I am asked where I am from, I say I'm Canadian. Montreal is my hometown, with all its chaos and excitement, all its language battles, its solitudes. When I think of home, that is the island I think of. If identity is traced to the place you were born, then I'm in trouble. My memories of Britain are scattered, and I feel no sense of belonging there. But blended into my Canadian experience is Caribbean culture: when I feel like an outsider in Canada, my parents' Caribbean roots keep me planted; they give me a sense of myself in the world. It's odd to relate to two sets of people, to live in two worlds, each world with its own nuances, traditions and beliefs. Balancing the Caribbean and Canadian is an incredible and exhausting act.

I know Barbados best of all. It was to that island that my sister and I would travel to meet relatives and spend three-week vacations in the 1970s. My first visit was in 1965. We sailed from England, on a voyage that seemed to take forever. Almost everyone got seasick. Later, on the bumpy ride to my grandparents' home, I told my mother that I was amazed by the number of trees. I was a city girl and, for me, Barbados, with all its fine flora, was one huge garden paradise. I fell in love.

While my father is Jamaican, I didn't actually go there until 1990. Despite that fact, most White Canadians seem to think Jamaica is where I belong. I say so because, after they ask me where I'm from, they quickly ask where my parents are from. My first answer is not what they are looking for. Barbados goes unnoticed. Jamaica rings a bell.

~~~

*Day two. This is incredible! I've sunk deeply into a great book. The hotel is nice, although the room is kinda small. Who cares? I'm spending perhaps too much time in the sun, my book in one hand, a rum punch in the other. Last night, I hung out at the hotel's outdoor variety show, all local talent, some singing and dancing, a skit, a magic act — not in the least bit Las Vegas, but something to do when the sun's gone down. I had grabbed another rum punch and was heading for a table in the back when I was summoned.*

*"Yoo-hoo! Come sit with us."*

*"No, no. I'm fine, really ..."*

*"No, please. You're always by yourself." I'd like to keep it that way, I thought, but said, "Okay, fine. Thanks!"*

*"I've been dying to ask you, what do you call those?" She pointed to my hair.*

*"Dreads," I said. "Dreadlocks."*

*"Oh my! It's very attractive," said her companion.*

*"Thanks."*

*"So how do you wash it? How long did it take to grow? Can I touch it?" She was gushing.*

*"Pardon?"*

*"You see, we're from Wasaga Beach and we never see Black people up there."*

~~~

It is funny, this belief that most, if not all, Black people in Canada can be traced to Jamaica, but to think otherwise would demand a greater knowledge of geography, knowledge that extended far beyond narrow assumptions and the headlines screaming from the newspapers.

The offense is not that of Jamaica. It's as good a place as any to be from. But there is resistance to accepting that Black people can be from Canada or elsewhere. Where does that leave Black Canadians who have been here for generations, in some cases longer than White Canadian families? How do Black Canadians feel about being linked to an island, a community, a region of the world, with no relevance for them? How long do we have to be here to be considered "Canadian"?

It seems Black people never will be.

Look for Black history in the core history texts. Talk to Canadians who still believe there was never slavery here. They haven't been shown otherwise. Black History Month helps to inform, but is it enough? I'm still asked where I'm from, my response still ignored. If I trace my roots to Jamaica, I give my questioners peace of mind, give them something solid to hold onto, but it keeps me an outsider, says I am not a "true" Canadian, means I don't belong here.

I never mention England when I'm asked where I'm from. Instead, I find myself volunteering my parents' roots when "Canadian" doesn't hold. If it makes the questioners feel better, I can be Bajan or Jamaican. It ends the discussion. Their strange curiosity is finally satisfied. They put me in my place; I show them the way.

But these roots only go so far. I was not easily accepted by Caribbean-born friends I met in high school, or at the CEGEP, or at university, or at work, because I just couldn't join in their conversations. They spoke of home: their old schools, the things they missed, their communities and events, the politics, the way of life. Their perspectives on the world were different from mine. Even getting used to the speech of various islands took patience and concentration. The first time I heard a Trinidadian speak, I was in awe. I kept asking him to slow down or to repeat what he was saying. That embarrassed me. That was what White Canadians would do, I thought.

~~

*I'm on a city tour today of Trinidad, an old city in the heart of Cuba. Time stands still here. People say that a lot about Cuba, but the proof of it is in this city, in the cobbled streets, the clapboard houses, the tiled floors inside the spacious dwellings. The houses can fool you. On the outside the paint is peeling, the wood worn and tired, but inside, the remnants of an earlier time fill the homes: beautiful, hand-crafted furniture, antique pieces from Spain and other parts of Europe. The original owners have long since fled the country. The women and men who cooked and cleaned these homes have "inherited" them and their interiors. Now, the properties are handed to their descendants.*

*It's been a good tour. Our guide, Juanita, is informative. I'm paired with a Canadian couple, so I don't have to worry about language, should I wish to strike up a conversation, but I'm distracted by my morning altercation with a German tourist.*

*He asks me, in Spanish, how long it will take for us to travel from our hotel to the town of Trinidad. I can't speak Spanish, but I can just make out what he asks me, so I explode and tell him, in English that I'm not Cuban. I'm Canadian. And yes, there are Black people in Canada.*

*It was totally inappropriate, I know. But it's day four, and after days of "Can we get an ashtray over here, por favor?" "You speak English? Is there any way of getting an extra towel?" "How long have you been working at this hotel?" "So what's it like living in Cuba?" I'm thoroughly pissed off.*

*Those same people waited in the lounge with me before we boarded the plane that brought us here. They think that I am Cuban because I am Black. I'm the only Black tourist at this hotel, the only Black person visiting from Canada. If the other tourists would stop drinking the country out of rum and bad beer they might notice that at this hotel, that in Cuba, only Cubans of Hispanic origin work in the positions requiring direct contact with tourists. The few Black Cubans that I have seen peek out from the cafeteria's kitchen during our meals. The Cubans I have met have been less than hospitable. No smiles for me, just a nod to indicate they'll take my drink order. Finally. Long, inquisitive looks as I pass by. Race continues to be an issue in Cuba, but it is subtle. At this hotel, because I'm the only Black tourist here, no one notices the racism but me.*

～～～

Identity has always been paramount for me. It was, for the most part, an issue I pondered on my own. After all, who could I talk to about it? My parents? Their focus has been on immigration: years of trying to leave their home countries, then getting settled, then assimilating into the culture of their newly adopted home. As far as they knew, their children would be spared demoralisation and humiliation. They would be afforded equal opportunities and a chance at a higher education. There was no way for my parents and their peers to anticipate an environment that would be hostile towards their children or to foresee school years plagued with racist practices. They didn't see the schoolbooks depicting Black people as subservient, ignorant people, the men carrying spears and the women bare-breasted. What could they know about having no sense of belonging?

For my Caribbean-born friends, my preoccupation with identity is puzzling. The question of where they are from is followed by a simple answer. They don't necessarily see why it is a loaded question for me or why it erases my sense of belonging. At the same time, when Caribbean people ask me where I'm from, my answer is always met with a sigh and, even with them, for the sake of wanting to belong, when I mention my parental background, it is with hesitation. I don't want their follow-up questions to be too probing because I have few answers. Their islands are known to me by extension. I'm just a slightly more informed tourist.

For years I have felt caught in the middle. On the one hand, there is the Barbadian-Jamaican side of me: the love of Caribbean foods, the islands them-selves, the music and history. On the other, there is Canada: the love of this land, its events, politics and struggles, all of which have shaped my life and beliefs, the land of all my accomplishments and disappointments thus far.

While I'm still in the middle of both worlds, I now take comfort in know-ing I am not alone. There are thousands of us, the children of immigrants, bouncing back and forth between two worlds, trying to find a secure place for ourselves between them. I find that I seek these people out and they me. When we meet there is no preamble, no "Where are you from?" No "Your parents?" No "Why do you speak like a Canadian?" There is acceptance. Finally. But these are mostly people of colour. With White Canadians, the struggle continues. It is difficult, if not impossible, to get them to stop asking the question, let alone to understand why it is exclusionary. Perhaps it's because to understand and act on my wish would mean erasing any trace of their privilege, would mean seeing me as I truly am: a Canadian. Period.

~~~

*I'm on my way back to my room after having supper with a group of women who spoke endlessly but had nothing to say. Tomorrow is my last day in Cuba and, aside from the racist crap from my fellow tourists and from the hotel staff, the holiday has been fine. I've finished my book and, after days of bathing in the sun, the winter chill seems to have finally left me.*

*"Turning in?"*

*"Yes." Sitting at one of the tables by the pool is a man with a number of beer cups around him. "How about a nightcap?"*

*Here we go again. "No, thanks. Kinda tired."*

*"Oh, c'mon. One drink ... c'mon."*

*"Fine."*

*I give him my order and he wobbles over to the pool bar. I suspect these all-inclusive packages must have some arrangement with Betty Ford-like clinics. You check out of here and into a clinic for rehabilitation. I've never drunk so much, and yet keep drinking because it's "free." My nightcap partner seems far ahead of me though; his beer cups are empty. When he returns he adds two more cups filled with beer to his collection and hands me my rum punch. His eyes are red from too much sun and drink. He really shouldn't be wearing shorts, but he is. Odd-shaped legs. His shirt is open and his beer belly rests comfortably on his thighs.*

I sip my drink and stare over at the other tourists jerking around frantically on the dance floor to some American techno-disco "music." He hasn't said anything to me since he sat back down, and I'm beginning to wonder what's going on when he blurts out, "I love this country."

I look around at the palm trees bending as if in slow motion to a warm evening breeze. "Ummm. Yes, there are some pluses."

"I mean, I don't care if it's communist, socialist ..."

"Well, I gotta get going ..." I cut him off. I really don't have time for this.

But he ignores me. "What I'm saying is, why can't Canada be like this?"

This is intriguing.

He continues, "Here in Cuba, everybody's living in harmony. All colours. Why can't Canada be like Cuba?"

"It is."

I get up and go to my room.

**Susan Lee**

# Identity

I question my own
renaming
and redefining
who I am
according to
"dominant" standards
Constantly reminded
we are all
Canadian
if we are white
no matter
what our past or
history or
how many generations
we are not
if we are not
white
Constantly being asked
where are we from
positions of privilege
allow that right
and many are offended when
I challenge the question
I've had enough of
"guess my nationality"
Raised in Canada
born in Japan

Westernised but non-Western
between and betwixt
two cultures
but neither
In "foreign" ground
and territory
it leaves me to
define myself
my way
A non-Western
but Westernised
Asian lesbian
who constantly struggles
to maintain
her space,
voice
and self

**Barbara Malanka**

# A Gem of Great Price

I have been asked often about my nationality: who my parents were, what ethnic group I belong to, what languages I speak. Some people are quite adamant about knowing these things, and I've always wondered why. Would I be given more respect, fired, passed over, disliked, despised, assaulted or shot if I gave an unacceptable answer? Is it better to be one thing and not another? Experience has taught me that the answer to these questions is yes. It is difficult to explain to someone with White skin the reasons for my hesitant or evasive answers. I have learned to be careful. I am who I am, but others are more comfortable thinking I fit nicely into some preconceived category as a mixed-race woman. "Oh, you're mulatto!" they gush, satisfied. But what lays behind that satisfaction, and how do tell them I find the term "mulatto" extremely offensive?

It is impossible for me to speak of identity without reflecting on all that I am. There is a duality in me: the part that is Black and the part that is White. But to say that I am a mixed-race woman is simplistic. It does not capture my experience or the reality in which I must live. I cannot use race as the only benchmark for my identity, for to do so would deny other aspects: the class, the languages and the cultures in which I was raised.

Let's begin with class. My White grandparents raised nine children in rural northern Ontario during The Depression. They lived in a house with no running water, no indoor toilet, and they burned wood for heating and cooking. My grandmother ran a beanery during World War II and took care of her children while my grandfather worked for the Ontario Northern Railway. My mother was the only girl in her family to finish grade eight — my grandfather didn't believe in educating girls; to him, it was a waste of time. My mother left home and, while working at a bakery during the day, completed high school at night.

She also learned to type and to take shorthand, skills that allowed her to leave northern Ontario and work in Montreal, Toronto and, finally, New York City where she met my father. She was one of the "Whites of good conscious" who lived, worked and socialised with non-Whites. Marrying my father was her way of proving her commitment to the ideal that "all men are created equal." How naïve she was.

My father was Black, born in the Carolinas and raised in Washington, DC. He was drafted into the US Navy and achieved the highest rank an unskilled Black man could achieve during the war — he was a cook. We lived in New York housing projects; in those days there were not many places a Black man could live with his White wife and baby. The playground I toddled around in was strewn with broken glass, rotting trash, faeces and urine.

What does it mean to be poor or working class? For me, it means living a life of want, knowing what it is like to go to bed hungry, appreciating second-hand clothes, working at any type of job in order to survive, making a pound of hamburger stretch over two meals, sharing the little you have because there is always someone who has less, learning that the intent behind a gift far out-weighs its price, knowing that, no matter what, you do survive.

Language and culture go hand in hand for me. There is a duality in that as well. My first language was French, but I spoke English at school and with my father's friends. I straddled two worlds: the French Canadian milieu of my moth-er's family and the world of southern American Blacks. In my mother's world I learned to bake butter tarts and tortière, to find pleasure in fishing and berry-picking, to fear God and the influence of the Church, to kick up my heels in a lively reel, to take pride in our language and to hate "les maudit anglais" who would steal it from us.

In my father's world I learned to cook grits and collard greens in salted pork rinds, to cheer the rise of Black baseball players in the major leagues, to laugh and clap in the house of God, to sing the blues, to hold my head high and never forget that the freedoms I enjoy today came after great sacrifice.

When I was about nine years old, my parents split up and my mother moved us to Canada. Very soon after we arrived in Ottawa, the phone calls began. Once I answered the phone and heard a word I'd never heard before: nigger. We would hear strange noises in the night and wake up to find garbage strewn over our lawn or our windows smeared with broken eggs. For the first time in my life,

I was afraid. I would cry myself to sleep remembering my father's stories of night riders and was sure one night we would discover a burning cross on our front lawn. I did not learn fear and intimidation in the ghettos of New York. I did not suffer humiliation and assault in the alleys of the Bronx. I learned to be fearful and suffered assault in the capital of the world's "most tolerant" nation. Those experiences are part of who I am. They are part of my culture.

I am uncomfortable being characterised by a single identity. I am a tapestry, with each thread made up of the sweet and bitter. I am café au lait and warm sweet potato pie, steaming hot grits smothered in maple syrup. I am poor but I carry a priceless legacy. I am a gem of great price.

## Joyce Brown
# Responses for Resistance

**HERE** are some *Responses for Resistance* I have devised over the years to answer that infamous question: where do you come from?

### Literal Response

STRANGER: "Where do you come from?"

ME: "My mother's womb." (End of conversation.)

### Genealogical Response

STRANGER: "Where do you come from?"

ME: "Well, I was born in Hamilton. My father, Stephen Brown, was born in Brantford. My paternal grandfather, Gordon Brown, was born in Brantford. My great-grandfather, Andrew Brown, was born in Dunnville. My great-great-grandfather, Stephen Brown, was born in Fort Erie. His father escaped across the border to Canada in a buggy ..."

STRANGER: "Will this take very long?"

ME: "My paternal great-grandmother, Agnes Morey, was born in Burfords. My great-great-grandfather, John Morey, was a free slave who came from New York. My great-great-grandmother was Elizabeth Brant, the daughter of Joseph Brant. My great-great-great-grandfather was a Mohawk Indian born in Ohio. Joseph Brant was also known as Thayendanega.

My paternal grandmother, Lorna Selby, was born in Brantford. My great-grandmother, Irene McComus, was born in Cayuga. She was of Irish descent. My great-grandfather, George Selby, was born in Woodstock. His parents' first names are unknown, but his mother's maiden name was Peterson ..."

STRANGER: "That's nice, but ..."

ME: "My mother, Cora Lawson, was born in Freemont, Saskatchewan. My grandfather, Joseph Lawson, was born in Oklahoma. My great-grandfather, Sam Lawson, was also born in Oklahoma. My great-grandmother was of Irish descent. My maternal grandmother, Eva Williams, was born in Toro, Oklahoma. My great-grandmother, Cornelia Reed, was born in Liberty Hill, Texas. My great grandfather, Charles Williams, was born in Moorville, Texas ..."

STRANGER: "Sorry. I thought you were from the West Indies." (End of conversation.)

## Island Strategy Response

STRANGER: "Where do you come from?"

ME: "The island of Canada." (End of conversation.)

## Logical Response

STRANGER: "Where do you come from?"

ME: "All Blacks are not West Indian. All West Indians are not Black." (End of conversation.)

## Politically-Correct Response

STRANGER: "Where do you come from?"

ME: "Africa, America, Canada." (End of conversation.)

## Philosophical Response

STRANGER: "Where do you come from?"

ME: "Evolutionists would argue that homo sapiens descended from apes. On the other hand, others would say Adam and Eve." (End of conversation.)

## Theological Response

STRANGER: "Where do you come from?"

ME: "We are all God's children." (End of conversation.)

## Coming-and-Going Response

STRANGER: "Where do you come from?"

ME: "From where I'm coming from. And if you don't leave me alone, you won't get to where you're going." (End of conversation.)

## In-a-Hurry Response

STRANGER: "Where do you come from?"

ME: "Work. I just left there a few minutes ago." (End of conversation.)

## Absenting-Oneself Response

STRANGER: "Where do you come from?"

ME: "Excuse me, I just remembered something I forgot."
(End of conversation.)

## Indignant Response

STRANGER: "Where do you come from?"

ME: "Canada."

STRANGER: "No, where were you born?"

ME: "Are you calling me a liar?" (End of conversation.)

## Reversal Response

STRANGER: "Where do you come from?"

ME: "Canada. Where do you come from?"

STRANGER: "Canada."

ME: "No, where do you really come from?" (End of conversation.)

## Homegirl Response

STRANGER: "Where do you come from?"

ME: "Canada.'"

STRANGER: "No, where were you born?"

ME: "Oh, I get it. I'm a homegirl. After my aunt delivered me, the ambulance took my mother and me to the hospital." (End of conversation.)

## Cut-Right-Through-the-Crap Response

STRANGER: "Where do you come from?"

ME: "Okay, just tell me where you went on holiday?"
(End of conversation.)

## Silent Response

STRANGER: "Where do you come from?"

ME: (Silence.)

STRANGER: "Where do you come from?"

ME: (Smile.)

STRANGER: "Do you speak English?"

ME: (Still smiling, but I shake my head to indicate no.)

STRANGER: "Sorry to bother you."

ME: "No problem." (End of conversation)

## Response with an Attitude

STRANGER: "Where do you come from?"

ME: "Look, you don't really care where the hell I come from. You see some Black person on the street and, bold as brass that you are, you get all up in my face. I could be from Mars. Why don't you ask this woman sitting beside us on the bus where she comes from? You don't have to answer that. Do you see me asking everyone I meet that question? Well, let me tell you where I went on vacation: Holland. Three snaps in your face." (A definite end to any conversation.)

## Michelle Scott
# Untitled

I have a major peeve with people who ask, "Where are you from?"or "Are you from Jamaica?" When I say, "No, I was born here, in Canada," there is always the second inevitable question: "Where are your parents from?" I do not see how my family tree or a Caribbean geography lesson is of relevance or even any of their business. It does not seem to matter how long you have been here: people still want to know where you come from. Does knowing that make you any more or less than what you are?

I have never asked anyone where they were from, and I have known people of many cultures and races; most of them emigrated from different countries. Where they came from may come up as a part of their heritage, but you are not solely defined by the place you were born. It is important, but being asked if I come from somewhere other than Canada always feels like a put down to me; it is as though Black people or people of any other visible minority group could not possibly have been born in Canada. Is Canada a country solely of White people? Where did this narrow-minded view come from? For a country that is supposed to pride itself on its cultural mosaic, there are too many people interested in proving how non-Canadian you are.

*"I was fifteen before I was actually in a room of Black people*
*and I was very uncomfortable."*

~ STRUGGLE FOR IDENTITY:
Seven Black Canadian Women Share Their Experiences

TWO

Fitting In

**Anurita Bains**

# Riding the Hyphen

**AFTER** I secured a summer job a few years ago, my boss invited me and the other employees out to lunch. It was June, so I showed up in shorts and a T-shirt. The lunch was basically a getting-to-know-you event and I didn't think much about it afterwards, that is, until a friend of mine who had also been there told me about a discussion she had later with my boss.

"Do you think Anne would be more comfortable doing tours in her traditional dress?" my boss asked. "Because, if she wants, she can do them in a salvaar chemise."

Her remarks, while infuriating and upsetting, aren't really that surprising. I have become accustomed to being defined by stereotypes by those who purport to know me or something about me. Although there is no doubt that my boss had seen me — during the interview and at the casual lunch — her comments clearly illustrated she hadn't really seen me at all.

Though I eventually became angry, my initial reaction was defensive. Did I look and act like someone who would wear a salvaar chemise? Hadn't she seen that I was wearing shorts and Doc Martens? Hadn't she noticed that my short haircut — usually one of the first signs of a non-practising Sikh, or at least of a rebellious one — was more than a fashion statement? Did I look that Indian?

How could such simple remarks rouse such complex feelings in me? I have yet to reconcile my South Asian culture and history with my "Canadian" upbringing. But how could my boss know that her attempt at liberal sensitivity would provoke a crisis in me? I guess it's no surprise: I have gone through my whole life trying to prove how "Canadian" I am.

I am four years old and I sleep through most of the seemingly endless flight to Canada. As soon as we arrive, my father and brother get their hair cut short — and so does my mother. The turbans are buried deep in the closet. We are abiding by the cardinal rule: look, be, act Canadian.

"Learn English," I am told, so I learn as quickly as I can because all I can remember is my torturously strict convent nursery school in India, where bad girls were dragged by their braids and bad boys got the ruler. I am so preoccupied with learning English that I forget Punjabi — something I later regret.

I am enrolled in school and registered as Anne, an anglicised version of my name. This, I am told, will save me from embarrassment in the classroom when my name is called during attendance-taking.

My parents work and go to school, so I spend a lot of time at home alone. I pass the time by watching television and napping, and while an hour seems to last a lifetime, I teach myself how to answer the phone, take messages and make crafts. I later realise my independent nature developed because of all the time I stayed at home by myself.

I am mastering this "Canadian" thing: any hint of an accent is gone, I have a "normal-sounding" name and kids to play with. I fit in. Unless someone explicitly asks, "Where are you from?" I can conceal that I am not Canadian, but a Canadian citizen from India, and aside from the odd "paki" or "chocolate milk" slur, I fare pretty well on the playground.

A year after a summer vacation in India, an Air India flight goes down over the Atlantic. "Did we know anyone on it?" I ask my parents. Of course we did. Everyone knew someone, I am told.

~~~

High school. We are now living in one of the richest towns in Canada, although my family is not rich. The town is also one of the WASPiest towns in Canada. In a high school of over 1,200 students, my brother, sister and I are three out of a handful of Indian kids.

We are over-achievers and over-involved. Race doesn't seem to be an issue. How can it be when many of the parents of our White friends are more proud of us than they their own children? My Indianness is virtually invisible.

Every once in a while my sister and I plead with my mother to let us wear "Canadian" clothes (whatever that means) when we go to Indian community functions. On the odd occasion when we lose that battle, we implore my father not to take the car out of the garage before we get in, lest the neighbours spot us dressed up in our elaborate outfits.

Every few months my parents tell us that only Punjabi will be spoken at home. My brother and I repeat meaningless phrases in Punjabi. My parents' valiant attempt doesn't last a day and even they revert to English as quickly as we do.

I go on my second summer vacation to India and impress my relatives with my extensive knowledge of apartheid and South Africa. My aunt tells me that India has its own form of apartheid. I do not understand what she means.

~~~

Fast forward to university. It's like waking from a long, deep and blissful sleep.

I get my nose pierced and everything seems to change. A simple nose pin has made it easier for others to pin down who they think I am or should be. On campus — aside from the occasional "That's gross!" or "Did it hurt?" — I am hoisted to cool, hip, activist status. (And to think all it took was a little body mutilation.)

I am no longer invisible but instead over-exposed. How many quotas, survey and committee requirements will I fill? How many liberal consciences will my presence ease?

I feel constantly bombarded by surveys in the media (the Globe and Mail is particularly prompt at reporting such "news") saying the majority of Canadians want immigrants to assimilate. I'm an immigrant. What am I supposed to do? Assimilate more? "They don't mean you," someone tells me. "You're not an immigrant. You're Canadian."

It's not enough any more for me to say that I am Canadian. No innate sense of pride overwhelms me with that statement — no chills down my spine, no special history or traditions that cross my mind. If I tell someone over the phone, "I am Canadian," what image is conjured up? On its own, it's an empty identity.

It is a relief when I meet and become friends with a woman who also feels lost, confused and isolated. It is as if a burden has been lifted. There is no need to explain the "background" when we exchange stories. I feel as if I have known her my entire life.

We tell each other stories about being in class and having certain expectations placed on us because our Indian identity is the first and only thing people see.

I am supposed to have a deeper understanding of Anita Desai and Salman Rushdie novels because the novels take place where I was born. But the truth is, I relate more to Hanif Kureishi's short stories and to movies made by second-generation South-Asian Canadians, where characters are pinned in a space between their parents' traditions and their immediate environment, than I do to tales of colonialism and imperialism. It is in the former works that the predicament of floating in an undefined space is discussed with the seriousness and complexity it deserves. Having my experience reflected in a book or on the screen gives me courage and confidence, it is comforting, it legitimises an experience that is usually difficult to articulate, and it substantiates what most people refuse to admit exists.

What others don't realise is that mine is an identity and a culture in the making. It's recognizing that both where I come from and where I am form my identity, and it's about being neither invisible nor over-exposed. It's about understanding that identity needn't have to be about fitting into someone else's mould or definition. If I can't be a part of the South-Asian community in Canada because they think I'm "too Canadian," and I don't quite fit into the mainstream Canadian culture, then I must seek and cultivate a community with others who realise that their identity won't be compromised for the sake of those who find it necessary to label and define us as something we are not.

As hyphenated Canadians we are somewhere in the middle, riding the hyphen, and we must create our own cultures, our own identities and tell our histories and stories with our own voices.

I feel sick when I think of the lengths I and many others have gone to, to assimilate, to fit in, but I guess it's no surprise because no one wants to stand out. But there was no real reason, no justification. It was just something you did — no questions asked.

### Lisa Valencia-Svensson

# It Never Sits Quite Right

always trying to make it work
always trying to fit
but it never sits quite right

Time stretches one long line
spreading cross and through

and I'm trying to squeeze my jelly life
into someone else's mould
little pieces always slipping out
or the whole mess slithering
to the floor with one resonant glop

and I'm always trying to make it work
always trying to fit
but it never sits quite right

Always trying to make it to work
and keep moving round the clock

trying to squeeze my sun-warmed self
into Protestant perversion
wrapping grey cement timelines
'round my rough tropical realities
the dissonance clashing in my mind

yet I keep on trying to make it work
I keep on trying to fit
though it never sits quite right.

### Annette Clough

# Snapshots in Sepia

**ON** my wall is a small photograph taken in Jamaica in the first decade of this century. It shows my maternal great-great-grandmother, Annie MacBlaine, daughter of slaves, wife of John MacBlaine, an Englishman. With her is my grandmother, two of her daughters and her sister. My grandmother was Sarah Louise Escoffery; Escoffery is a name that originated in Haiti. She is married to Alfred Parke, with the blue eyes my sister inherited. The Parkes, if the point were pressed, would identify as Brown Jamaicans. This is all I know about them.

The history of my father's family is even less known. The Cloughs came from England generations ago. My grandmother was apparently Jewish or part Jewish (in Jamaica that means Sephardic Jews). No one admitted to any African ancestry. The Cloughs thought of themselves as White.

I was born in 1941 into a family that was mixed race for generations. However, it was never discussed as such. What mattered to them was shade of skin and the level of society that shade entitled you to. Class and race were inseparable in people's minds and the terms were often used interchangeably. Assumptions were made about people's class, based on appearance, even though in the same family one child might have quite dark skin and another might be light enough to be called White. I heard stories of mothers telling their darker children that they would never have the privileges of their lighter-skinned siblings. I learned that skin colour and shades of skin colour said who you were, what you could do, where you could go and how you should be treated.

## 1946

My family goes away to a beach cottage for a month. I come home deeply tanned. The two English children from across the road, children I used to play with, are told they cannot play with me any more because I am too dark. I am bewildered.

As I grow up, the idea that White equals better becomes deeply entrenched. I choose light-skinned children as my friends. Not surprisingly, my father knows their fathers. This changes in my teens: many of my friends that I meet at school are dark skinned; my father does not know their fathers. I begin to gain some perspective on history and colonialism and where ideas about race and class come from. I barely understand how much privilege the accident of my skin colour gives me.

## 1953

My family goes to New York. We meet my father's half-brother for the first time. He runs a hotel for Black people in upstate New York. He looks just like my father, but in America he is considered Black. I do not understand.

In the early sixties I come to Canada to attend art college and then university. I hang out with other foreign students. Identity seems to mean country of origin and students from the Caribbean identify with their island. I identify as Jamaican. To White Canadian students, I am exotic. This is my first experience of "otherness," but it is not painful. My privileged background has given me assumptions about my equal status in White Canadian society, and I do not see being made into something exotic as the subtle form of racism that it is.

When I go home after my first winter in Canada, looking pale and wan, my grandmother is delighted that my skin has "cleared up so nicely." She is horrified that I rush to lie in the sun and regain my tan. I can hardly wait to look like my old self again.

## 1967

I emigrate to Canada after seven years of going back and forth between Canada and Jamaica. I had always expected to go home after getting my degree, but I find myself back in Toronto, not really understanding why I am making the choice. It takes a long time to figure out that in Toronto I feel much freer to be myself, whatever that is. In Jamaica I feel incredibly restricted by the assumptions made because of my family name, my accent and, of course, my skin. In Toronto no one criticises my choice of friends, or jobs, or clothes or activities. With this freedom, though, comes new levels of understanding. I come to see that the other side of privilege in Jamaican society is a profound alienation from the culture of the majority of the people. It is easier for me to fit into Canadian society than it is for me to be part of what I consider the real Jamaica, the Jamaica of the majority of its people. But when I get my Canadian citizenship, I cry. I'm not a Canadian, but what am I?

# 1975

International Women's Year. A Jamaican friend asks me to become involved with planning Black Women's Day as part of the Month of the Woman Artist. I am honoured and accept without hesitation. I "come out" as Black, so to speak. I am part of a group of Caribbean, Canadian and American Black women and become friends with an American woman. She and my White American boyfriend argue about whether or not I am Black. He says I am not culturally Black as he understands it; she says I am racially Black and therefore am Black. I'm confused. Is identity based on race or culture? And who is asking the question — me or the society around me?

In the eighties I live in Vancouver and become active in the women's movement. Race is now an issue for feminists, but I am often invisible. Women who think they are aware of racism talk about "our all-White collective" while I am sitting there. When I correct their mistake, the subtext of their apology is clear: you are so much like us, we forget. I do not, but I cannot oppose that thinking strongly because I am still unsure about who I represent. I have no connection to the small Caribbean community in Vancouver. I do find identity in the now common term "woman of colour." It seems more honest in a sense for me than "Black woman," as my heritage is less than fifty percent African.

# 1986

A friend and I start a group for women of colour. I go to a meeting and a Black woman from Trinidad says to me, "What are you doing here? I thought this was only for women of colour?" More confusion. Is my identity what I appear to be or what I know I am? Is my claiming the identity of Black woman or woman of colour offensive to women who are very visible and very much the target of oppressive behaviour in ways that I am not? Or is it seen as solidarity in a racist society?

Now I am living in Toronto again, not much connected to the Caribbean after years away, and struggling in these times of identity politics to figure out what identity means to me. In Jamaica we have so many names for different shades of skin and racial mixes that I would be laughed at for calling myself Black. In the either/or world of racial politics in Canada, I am expected to be Black or White. Politically, then, I'm Black. But what is identity about — race, culture, visibility or political solidarity? All of these, I suppose, but there's more. Identity is also about community, but as a mixed-race, Caribbean, lesbian with a White partner, parenting a White child, what is my community?

I'm having trouble writing a conclusion to this piece because I don't know what conclusions to draw. I do know that identity means something more personal and profound than the labels I claim of necessity because I live in this time and place. I have come to value the perspective that seeing issues from many sides can bring. My work now, both personally and politically, is about making connections and building bridges of understanding; it is not about fragmenting and polarizing — society is already doing that to us. My hope is that wherever I go, however I identify, whatever community claims me, I can go confidently, knowing I am being true to myself, by just being myself.

**Nadine Leggett**

# Struggle for Identity: Seven Black-Canadian Women Share their Experiences

# WHEN

I was four years old, I announced that I no longer needed my mother to walk me home from kindergarten. I explained to her that as a mature, responsible and independent kindergartner, I was quite capable of walking home by myself. The school being only two blocks from our home and visible from our front yard, my mother gave her consent to this new arrangement.

The next afternoon, as she watched anxiously for my familiar shape to make its way down the sidewalk, she was surprised to see me trotting along happily holding the hand of my playmates' mother, Mrs. Johnson. I explained to my mother that she, my mother, was White, but I was Black; Mrs. Johnson was Black and Black children had Black mothers. As a Black child adopted into a White family, that was when I first recognised that I was a different colour than the rest of my family and, moreover, that other families were not racially mixed in this way.

Trying to form a strong self-identity while being raised Black in a White community is fraught with conflict and struggle. The vital ingredients, such as culture, history and acceptance, are omitted from the most immediate environment. My own experience was complicated further by being a member of a racially-mixed family. For Black women, acquiring a healthy self-image in White Canadian society is a unique struggle in comparison to the other tribulations associated with growing-up: our place is not apparent, we have to define our place as we go along.

Seven Black-Canadian women, including me, came together to discuss our lives and our histories. We discussed our families, our schools and the communities that we call home. We are all educated young professionals between the ages of twenty-five and thirty. We share similar backgrounds: spending most of our developing years in Canadian cities and towns where Blacks were (and in most cases still are) a definite minority. There are, however, important differences which enriched our exchange of experiences. Our combined childhood communities include southern Ontario, Newfoundland and Nova Scotia.

Despite the differences, there were strong similarities which we quickly recognised. What follows highlights what we identify as the core issues associated with growing up as Black women in Canada.

## Community

*"I was fifteen before I was actually in a room*
*of Black people and I was very uncomfortable."*

Many of us developed a love-hate attitude towards the few other Black people living in our communities. There was a strong, sometimes overpowering, desire to reach out to other Blacks, but this was complicated by our awkwardness and unfamiliarity. Most of us confessed to having better relationships with White people.

"I didn't even know I was Black until I was seven years old," commented Cora, a woman who lived in Nova Scotia for most of her childhood. Apart from her family, there were no other Black people in her world. As a child she could not conceptualise what the differences were. Other children, however, readily made those differences clear. " I remember being in kindergarten ... some kid calling me 'nigger' and it meant nothing because I had never heard it before. He might as well have called me a pair of jeans."

People would take photographs of Cora's family for novelty's sake. Even from a young age she knew she was different somehow. She recalls that when she was seven years old a White male playmate told her, "My mother said that I cannot marry you because you are Black."

In Chatham, Ontario, established Black Canadians, having inhabited that area for generations after escaping slavery in the United States, discriminated against new immigrant Blacks. Dee, who went to high school in the area, recalls feeling resented by the Black-Canadian population. She did not feel a part of that group but somehow found greater acceptance from the White community.

However, for other women, the Black community in other areas, despite its small size, did provide support and comfort. Some of us were drawn to other Blacks and gravitated to places where we could seek out fellow Black Canadians. Locating others whose origins were the same as our parents' was not important; the primary factor was skin colour.

Jem and I both grew up in Burlington, Ontario. In our adolescent circle of friends, the nearby larger cities of Toronto and Hamilton were the places where we focused our sights for the future. We spent a lot of time forming a network with others from the larger cities, through friends, extended family and social events. At our high school, the Black kids from all the grades hung around together forming one cohesive group.

Tara was raised in Toronto. She is of mixed-race parentage but was adopted as an infant into a White family. Near her middle-class neighbourhood there was a low-income community where many Black families lived. Tara was not permitted to go to that area because it was perceived as being violent, but she secretly went there often. Beyond the temptation of entering forbidden territory, Tara thinks in retrospect that the main attraction was to be around other Black people. Tara's light skin tone did not allow her unlimited acceptance in the White community. She still felt the same degree of alienation and racism as other Black people.

Before Karen's family moved to Toronto, she spent her early childhood in Nova Scotia. Like Tara, Karen is of mixed-race parentage and "light-skinned." She has always thought of herself as being Black. However, she was rejected by her Black peers at school because she was racially mixed. She only felt accepted in White social circles.

Lynn, the seventh member of the discussion group, lived in a predominantly White suburb of Toronto. "I always wished for a very close Black friend," she confessed. Her world broadened when she left home to go to university. Once she had more contact with Black people at university, Lynn began to understand fully what had been missing in her life and why she had felt so alone.

## School

> "The only thing (about Black history) that I can remember
> them talking about at school is in geography.
> They would talk about Pygmies running around with spears ..."

We all agree that there was none to minimal Black history taught in our elementary or high schools. Any history of Black people would usually be about "primitive" cultures in Africa — and those cultures were presented as being completely barbaric — or have to do with some brief mention of the slave trade. During those lessons, any description of African women would include mentioning that they walked around bare-breasted and claims that Africans lived like animals. There wasn't anything admirable about their ways of life. They did not even appear exotic. We dreaded the subjects of Africans being raised in class because we knew the embarrassment that would result. Whoever was chosen to read from the text book would invariably pronounce the Niger River as the "Nigger River." As one or the other of us was usually the only Black person in the class, we all remembered wishing the floor would give way and swallow us whole.

Faced with such a negative representation of African people, we were driven to disassociate ourselves from our own heritage. We convinced ourselves that as Black Canadians we were more sophisticated, more intelligent and definitely more "evolved" than the "savage" Pygmies presented to us in class. We thanked heaven we had been rescued from such a backward, ignorant existence and taught the White "normal" way of living. Sitting in a grade seven classroom, ready to explode with shame, feeling the gaze of twenty-six pairs of eyes, we would have preferred to have landed on earth in an alien vessel to being reminded of our crude ancestry.

Not one of us ever questioned the validity of what was being taught about Black history in school. The teachings seemed consistent with many other social reminders, including television. In addition, given the isolation of being the sole Black family in the community, there were no other models to show us how Black people from different cultures really lived.

Although both of Dee's parents were born and raised in Ghana, she says, "I knew what Africa was like, it wasn't just all those awful stereotypes ... Yet those things still affected me deeply ... comments about the hair, the lips, the butt. Even though it was counter-balanced by all the positive stuff I had at home, it still affected me very, very deeply."

Not only did we not learn anything positive about Black history but what we were taught was presented in a negative and uninteresting manner. There was no celebration of individual and cultural differences. Only as adults, on our own initiative, did we begin to see a more balanced and complete picture of our history. Our minds were opened and our attitudes changed dramatically as we entered adulthood and furthered our education. Lynn explains that at nineteen she felt a certain amount of pride about being Black but says she "wasn't into Black issues because I didn't know there were Black issues." She then felt resentful towards White people. She saw in university what high school could have been like with a greater number of Black students and with a curriculum that reflected the influence of various cultures.

*"My sister was told by the guidance counsellor that she would be best as a cook."*

Whether the discrimination was based on race, economics or gender, about half of the women interviewed say they or a family member were discouraged from pursuing higher education. A couple of the women believe strongly that the education system does not have any real interest in encouraging Black children to do well in school. Those students who show some difficulty are streamlined into general courses and average or above average students are actively discouraged from achieving scholastic success or meeting their potential.

Cora had a different experience. When she was growing up the education system in Newfoundland expected non-White children to excel academically. All the non-White families in her community were professionals. Cora believes this partly forced the people in her community not to have negative stereotypes of Black people.

But parental involvement is also an extremely important part of a child's academic success and the women in the group adamantly state that parents cannot fully trust any school system to place or teach their children appropriately.

# Family

*"I can remember my mother saying be strong, be proud."*

We received love, nurturing and caring from our families. Yet our parents had a fundamental lack of understanding about what we were going through. Although most of them shared our experience of being part of a visible minority, they had developed their own ways of dealing with those experiences. Their ways were different from the ones we would need to develop.

For the women like me who had been adopted into White families, our parents were even more removed from understanding our struggles. Parents who had been raised in predominately Black countries, such as in the Caribbean, were now focused on assimilating. Cora told us, "I think my mother wanted to use Patois with us. She stopped when we reached a certain age." Similarly, Lynn said that as a teenager, "When I talked Black pride they (her parents) got scared."

Our parents did not discuss Black issues or teach Black heritage at home. If they had, given all else we were exposed to, we might not have been able to accept the information.

Cora remembers not inviting her playmates home because they would notice the Black artwork on the walls and observe her father's Muslim practices. Cora confesses, "The things I felt uncomfortable about sharing were the things that connected me with being Black." The visual symbols in Cora's home represented a positive Black heritage, yet Cora struggled to distance herself from her Black world to fit in with her White friends. It was painful to live with the conflicting messages coming from our hearts and our heads.

Every member of the group identifies her mother as being her primary role model. Without question, we admire their strength, determination and stamina. Some of us believe strongly that the specific circumstances of being Black in a White world contributed to our mother's influence. Although, throughout our childhood we could admire the White heroines commonly seen in the media, racial distinctions prevented any significant identification.

## Hair

*"People would come over and I would be washing my hair and they would not understand that it is not going to take five minutes."*

A heartfelt communal groan erupts from the group at the onset of our discussion about hair. Waves of appreciative laughter accompany each vignette of hair trials and tribulations. Lynn tells us how hair tainted her annual summer camping experiences. No one else at camp understood why she dreaded swimming and getting her hair wet.

Wherever we went as children, White hands could not resist exploring our fuzzy mess of curls, braids or locks. Being young and painfully aware of the many physical differences between us and our peers, we followed the pattern of many Black women and tried expensive, extensive and sometimes quite painful means to transform our hair. These perms and relaxers sometimes backfired — scalps burned, hair fell out. Even of getting our hair done at a salon was a day-long event. Washing our hair at home was just as labour-intensive; it was reserved for weekends and took a half day at least.

With horror, we remember how we used to prance around with towels on our heads, pretending the towels were long flowing, golden hair. Jem recalls running upstairs to rip out her freshly corn-rowed hair after it had taken her mother hours to braid — Jem's friends had arrived unexpectedly at the door. Her mother's rage seemed a small price to pay to save herself the embarrassment of being seen in a distinctly Black hair style.

Our worry about our hair is only one example of how we rejected our Negro features. When we were growing up in the seventies and early eighties, full lips were considered big not pouty, music stars did not wear their hair in dreadlocks, and the afro was passé. Being Black was simply not in style.

## Dating

*"I didn't consider myself attractive*
*and I assumed that everybody else thought so too."*

Most pre-adolescents enter puberty and dating awkwardly and self-consciously. As Black women, we encountered obstacles that exacerbated a difficult initiation and integration into the dating world. "All my friends were White, but to date a White guy was hard," says Lynn. Getting along well in the classroom with White guys was one thing, but being considered a girlfriend was another. There was an invisible border that both sides were hesitant to cross.

As grown women, we could identify some of the causes behind those unspoken rules. On our side of the border, there was low self-esteem — we had internalised racism and turned it into self-hatred. As Cora points out, we saw ourselves as being unattractive and therefore invisible. Jem remembers being shocked at the idea that a White guy had even considered her attractive.

But when we did venture out on a date with a White guy we felt uncomfortable and self-conscious. We thought people were looking at us, judging us.

While we thought of ourselves restricted to dating Black men, some of us felt rejected from them as well. Dee explained that in Chatham Black guys dated only White girls. "Black guys would talk to you and be friendly ... but as far as (being their) significant other, you weren't in the picture." Because of that, Dee developed an aversion to her Black male peers and in high school decided to date White boys.

When as adults we moved to larger cities for employment and for university, the number of available Black men in our environments increased. Most of us started dating young Black men when we were in our late teens or early twenties. We slowly progressed to feeling comfortable about having romantic relationships with White men as well. We felt that it was not difficult to get along well with White men because we knew their world. They did not know ours, nor did we feel particularly motivated to share our world with them. There remained a residual attitude of masking our differences rather than enhancing them. That attitude was similar to our efforts to make ourselves invisible when we were children, and we found we used that same coping mechanism in our relationships with White men. Both sexism and racism influenced our belief that only by changing ourselves would we receive love, affection and respect from non-Black men.

## Where We Are Today

*"We are not where we should be,*
*but I believe we are making strides."*

Some of us have reached a balance in our personal lives. We have each become self-accepting and feel comfortably integrated into both White and Black worlds. Our lives include friends of many cultures and we feel pride in our heritage.

For Karen, striving to finding a balance continues. She could not join the Black community at all when she was young and she still has a strong desire to make that connection. In some ways it is even more difficult for her now. "Sometimes, I'm uncomfortable because I am so comfortable with White people. I feel trapped between two extremes."

Similarly, Tara, whose background is racially mixed, has not yet found the balance she wants in her life. She constantly categorises her social environment based on racial groupings. She limits her close friendships, interests and activities to those she considers to have a Black cultural orientation. Her world is divided into Black and White, without any grey.

> *"You get put in that role your whole life of always being*
> *the person who is the equaliser."*

Today, our hair is still considered public property for all who wish to touch it. We are asked to comment on topical issues, based on the assumption that we are spokespersons for the entire Black population. Negative images of Black people still pervade the mass media, disproportionately connecting our people to drugs, crime and corruption. And the institutionalised prejudices so apparent at school are now present at work.

As these new scars are added to the old, we find we are now stronger, wiser and better able to fight back.

**Dawn Carter**

# Short Reflective Essay #329

I'D like to grasp the cold earth in my hands and rub it into every crevice, every line that covers my palms so that the colour matches the back of my hands.

But the dirt is too brown.

Almost black.

If I dipped my hand in cinnamon, its scent in every pore, would it look like the rest of my body?

Cinnamon, nutmeg ... spicy, fragrant brown.

I was the brownest in that small town.

The only Brown person in all my classes. No one could beat my tan.

I wonder what they thought as day after day the one person who was physically different walked through the door every morning. A brown speck in a sea of white.

Why was I different?

I spoke the same language, there was no accent in my voice.

Did they wonder if I liked Black boys or White boys?

What if I had a crush on one of them? That couldn't be possible.

Would I be filled with contempt for their Whiteness?

Could I find one of their jokes funny?

Would I harbour within myself, a slew of White jokes and laugh hysterically to the punch-lines when no one else was around?

What did they think?

What did they think of me?

I don't remember smiling much. The only things that brought me pleasure were the green grass, the flowers of many colours, the smiles of my teachers who praised my writing and drawing.

Did they wonder why? Was my closed expression a reflection of my history?

Did the pain of past slavery and (recent) discrimination show in my eyes — arousing guilt?

Do they wonder where I came from?

My ancestors came from Africa. Now, we all come from Jamaica. That's where all Black people come from, isn't it?

So, how did so many of us come from such a small island?

Did we spring up from the brownness of the earth: some from the mountains amidst the coffee beans, some from the countryside among the sugar cane fields, others in city backyards from seeds planted at the base of coconut trees?

Did they see the blood that flowed when I fell and scraped my knees in the parking lot and the pinkish-white flesh that peeked through as I wiped the wound clean?

Maybe they thought I was a Vulcan, like Spock, who when wounded bled a bright fluorescent green and healed instantly, unlike any human being.

I remember my aunt using bleaching cream on her face to lighten,

brighten,
whiten
her features.

## Louise Bak

# b-seen

I've no particular place to go
just when I think
I am lost
sludging in four-foot snow-drifts
in undersized winter boots that
pinch in the cold stillness
constricting thoughts of fragrant soles
coddled
bare
in a mango-scented sampan
by a shore where sweat-shamans sat
with braids unchopped
until they reached the
faraway gold mountain(ers)
who beguiled hopeful searchers
with metal venality
connecting a land from sea to sea
which could not see
them then
or
me now
as expector general(isers)
mis-view
me on top of

Humpty Dumpty
in pieces
having fallen from The Great Wall
after a three-generational push
from the O'Canassimilators
pulp-fictioning my trajectoral cove
geographically far
but germinally close
in my life-tones
as I sip chrysanthemum tea with Diet Coke
better(fying) The Real Thing and
blenderizing the divisions away to
border-crossing balance.

*"Every time the teacher mentioned 'black,' 'apes,' or 'Africa,'*
*she would always look at me."*

~ WHERE BEAUTY SITS

# 3
## THREE

# Mirror, Mirror

**Lorena Gale**

# Where Beauty Sits

"**LET**" me be frank with you," she said, distractedly shuffling photos and résumés around her desk. "When you come right down to it, it really doesn't matter how talented you are. You have to have the right look. Unfortunately, you just don't have it. Most advertisers want attractive people beside their product. And to be quite honest with you," she looked at me as if I was about as appealing as a dog's breakfast, "I don't think you're very attractive."

Well, my chin dropped to my navel. I was so shocked. The casting agent was telling me to my face that she thought I was ugly.

"If something comes along that I think you are suited for," she added doubtfully, "I'll call you."

Now I must confess that I have always secretly believed that I was unattractive, a sad-looking child, girl-put-a-bag-on-your-head unattractive. I don't know why, but every time I'd ask my mother if I was pretty, she would say, "Nothing ugly lives near me. I don't have ugly children." Or my sister would say, "Lorena, you have strong features. Your face has its own unique beauty." I wasn't convinced.

I know this sounds like I'm being too hard on myself, but when was the last time you looked in the mirror? Aren't we all insecure about some aspect of our appearance?

~~~

I grew up in an area of Montreal called Outremont. We were one of two Black families living there in the days when Black people were said to have hair like steel wool and liver-lips. Anglo and Francophone children walked in packs behind us, chanting "nigger," "black," or "nigger black," as we made our way to school. In the schoolyard girls skipped to "Nigger, nigger come to dinner half past two ..." and everyone made difficult choices easier with "Eenie, meenie, miney, moe, catch a nigger by the toe ..." Even choosing teams for school games was hard, and we were lucky to be chosen at all.

I'd shrink into the shadows of the schoolyard with my best friend, Sybll, an East Indian girl to whom the aroma of exotic spices clung in a cloud of childhood stigma. All the kids insisted she smelled like pee. Wary of the knots of screaming children, wondering which warring gang would turn its malicious gaze upon us, we became watchful little soldiers, ever alert for any sign of attack. In the shadows we would sing in painful harmony, "Strawberries, cherries and an angel kissing spring ..." Safe, until the bell rang.

That was the early sixties. Civil rights were an American issue. Large-scale racial conflict was something that happened in the cities and backwaters of the American South, not in Canada. Here, you could eat at any restaurant — that would serve you. You could sit at the front of the bus beside a White person — but that didn't mean he or she wouldn't get up and move to a seat across the aisle. The Fair Accommodations and Practices Act of 1961 said you could live anywhere you could afford — that is, if you could persuade someone to rent or sell to you.

Malcolm X and Martin Luther King were still alive. Emmett Till wasn't so lucky. "Alabama" and "lynching" were words I would often overhear in adult conversations. Threatening words. Terrifying words. Words ripe with fear, rage, suspicion and hope gone sour. I discovered that the way I looked could evoke anger, hatred, even violence, in some people. However, I couldn't understand why. And that scared me.

Long before we chanted, "Say it loud, I'm Black and I'm proud," before the nationalist slogan, "Black is Beautiful," before the afro, the book, *Little Black Sambo* sat mockingly on a shelf in my classroom along with *Bunga of the Jungle*. Both made me squirm uncomfortably at my desk. Every time the teacher mentioned 'black,' 'apes,' or 'Africa,' she would always look at me.

"Colour," a teacher once said, "is not just the spectrum of hue perceived by the eye. Each colour, itself, has meaning. For example white means goodness, purity and light. Black is dark, dirty and evil."

I sat perplexed, at the centre of most classroom controversy and misconduct: passing notes, arguing with teachers, quarrelling with the other pupils, watching the snow fall and wishing I was someone else, somewhere else.

My sisters say I cried a lot as a child. I can't remember the tears as much as the confusion. Why didn't my teacher have the time to explain a difficult problem to me? Why didn't the other kids want me in their group for class projects or select me for a study partner? I was as smart as other kids in class.

That was the sixties and seventies in Outremont. Ignorant bigots like Archie Bunker in the television sitcom, "All in the Family," were pop culture icons. But what his character represented was considered dangerous by Black people. He portrayed racism as something to laugh at. We didn't find it funny. Black activists were arming themselves for change. There were riots, teargas and blood on the streets of America. Black consciousness was growing. Everyone seemed ready for change, yet change did not always mean progress. I remember my sister let her hair grow into an afro, but when she got a job as a go-go dancer on a local TV show she straightened it again. She even bought a long hair-piece that fell about her shoulders in a flip that bounced when she danced. Wow! I thought it made her look beautiful. I couldn't wait until I was old enough to have one of my own.

~~~

A gang of kids was waiting for me one day in the schoolyard. "What will you do now that your leader is dead?" they rumbled. What were they talking about? I didn't have a leader. I had thought mine was a solitary struggle. I ran home, afraid of what they might do to me, and found my mother slumped over the kitchen table, crying.

"They shot him. The bastards shot him." Her body was twisted with rage and she heaved with grief. I had never seen her so distraught.

"They couldn't lynch him, so they shot him. They shot him. Martin Luther King. They shot him dead on the ground." She was angry and bitter and the fierceness she always kept hidden was like fire in her eyes.

"Every time you try to rise up, they'll beat you down again. They'll try to rob you of your dignity. They'll try to steal your pride. But don't let them, you hear? Don't let them break your spirit. They'll try to take everything you have in this world just to keep you in your place. They'll even try to take your life. But there's one thing God gave you that's yours to keep forever. They can't take your soul, Lorena. Don't ever give away your soul. You hear me? I'm talking about survival in the White man's world ...

Don't give up no matter how hard it gets. Keep reaching for the stars and you'll have the universe. We are coloured. And though your skin will seem like a weight around your body, don't let anybody tell you that you aren't beautiful and good. You are the future. You have a right to the future. Don't let anyone take that away from you."

## Vancouver 1990

As I sit across from the casting agent I am reminded of the advice my mother gave me that day. Now, as I look at her closely, at her bottled-blond hair and blue contact lenses, her oversized designer clothes, I smile. No wonder she can't see me. She can barely see herself.

## Jaya Chauhan and Melody Sylvestre

# To be Asian, Black and Brown: Questions of Identity

## Jaya Chauhan

I was born in Kenya thirty-six years ago. My parents were born in India. When I was twelve we moved to England. I lived there until my recent immigration to Canada. For the most part, Canadians tend to identify me as East Indian, a member of the visible minorities, or a woman of colour. In England I would be identified by some people as Asian. As a woman of Indian origin living in the diaspora, I have identified myself as a Black woman,"Black" as a political colour.

## Melody Sylvestre

Twenty-nine years ago I was born in India, in an Anglo-Indian community. The community was distinct from the dominant Indian population in that we were a minority group of Christians, a religion which emerged in India during the days of British colonialism. My parents moved to Canada when I was two years old and I have lived here since that time. I think that many people in Canada do not know how to classify me with respect to a cultural or ethnic background and, as a result, I remain uncategorised in terms of being "Brown," "Black" or "Canadian."

## Jaya Chauhan

I grew up in Nairobi, Kenya, in a traditional, Gujarati-speaking, Hindu, Indian household, with hierarchical relations of male superiority and female subordination. My parents emigrated from India to Kenya as British subjects, both India and Kenya being British colonies at the time. At one time, I uncritically defined myself as Indian-Asian. However, as my critical consciousness developed and I was able to name the gender, race and class practices that have shaped who I am in the world, I chose to identify myself as a Black woman. My examination of the educational promotion of multiculturalism and my critique of racist practices and perspectives motivate me to use "Black" as a concept that informs my everyday practice in a society that is organised to benefit various races, classes, genders and sexual orientations differently. In using "Black," I reshape a past that has destructively claimed me and from which I wish to be freed.

In the Gujarati language, which I grew up speaking, "white" is synonymous with "beautiful." The lighter your complexion, the greater the likelihood of your being considered beautiful by others. In my community (as in other cultures), appearance plays a key role in choosing a bride for marriage and, therefore, is a signifier of how one will fare in love, caring, relationships, marriage, the family, and so on. My complexion is dark, compared to my siblings and, in contrast to my siblings, I am not considered beautiful. I can still hear echoes of my mother describing me in unfavourable terms: I was not a beautiful baby or child or adult, but my sister was beautiful and therefore more worthy. I believe that affected my overall development and I now have internalised images of beauty based on racist and sexist assumptions. Furthermore, my surname gives away that I was born in a low-caste Hindu family, and there are memories of humiliation associated with that. We could provide services to others of high-caste, but they would not touch or eat food from us. Even today, in England, there is an Indian woman who uses my mother's sewing services but for whom eating or drinking in our household is taboo.

Because we were poor, every year when we lived in Kenya my mother had to beg the school principal to reduce our school fees. In my mind lurks the shame of being poor and low-caste. I think that this has diminished me in some ways and it saddens me that, even in the eyes of those with the same skin colour as me, I am viewed as being less than they are. In sharing these fragmented and uncertain meanings of my social history in this way, there is, at least in the West, the danger of being seen as exonerating colonialism. That is not my intent. Colonialism has played a major role in organizing people in the colonies on the basis of gender, caste, and class, perpetuating power relations and enabling the exploitation of land and resources. Furthermore, a racist discourse in the West continues to portray Asian women in stereotypes, as being submissive and oppressed when compared to their Western counterparts, rather than critically examining our commonalities and our differences.

In England I attended a multicultural school that did not celebrate differences. Rather, these were denied and negated. It was very common to be called a "paki," and I was given the nickname "Currybeans". My family, my community and the way I lived were devalued and disparaged. Growing up within a dominant non-Black culture, the hierarchy of racism is in my consciousness, and today it leads me to resent the use of "Brown" to describe me.

I am painfully aware that I was given the opportunity for an education and that some of my peers, overwhelmingly from the Caribbean, were confined to ESN (educationally sub-normal) classes, considered "dumb" and "stupid" and stereotyped as being "lazy" and lacking in ambition. I was paid more attention by my teachers, which, consequently, enabled me to pursue higher education. I know only too well that I have obtained my qualifications in an unequal society, where schools with no anti-racist perspective have failed an overwhelming majority of the minority members of our society.

I think that I am no more black than White people are white and that if I am a woman of colour, then does that mean that white is not a colour and that White women are devoid of colour and therefore special? I am disillusioned by others who resent my use of Black because they signal to me a significant distinction in how we understand the practice of racism in a society where difference is continually negated. My intent here is not to reify certain social identities but to speak from the chaos of my experience. For too long I have felt locked in a cage of self-doubt and self-denial and I need to make sense of the knots that tangle my spirit. At another time and in another social space, I might choose to identify myself in other ways, but the longer I live in Canada, where Black as a political colour has no established meaning, I see myself having to choose other identities.

Canada is one of the few industrialised nations in the West to develop a state policy of multiculturalism (Ujimoto, 1991). In my understanding, that has enabled the building of bureaucracies that serve the ruling elite in society and that perpetuate racism rather than subvert it. I am suggesting that as a people with a common struggle against racism, despite our different communities, histories and traditions, we are by the institutionalisation of multiculturalism pitted against each other, reproducing the social relations of power. The resistance of a people against racism as an institutional practice is thus deflected and diffused, leaving intact the structures that support racism.

In her study of women of African, Caribbean and Asian origins, Amina Mama (1989) asserts the use of Black

> ... rather than the other more cumbersome and equally problematic terms available (e.g., 'Black and ethnic minority women,' 'Third World women' or the American 'women of colour,' etc.). This reflects the political legacy of Black political organizing in the 1970s and early 1980s, in which the necessity for concerted and united action against racism and oppression in Britain was emphasised. Since that time there has been an orchestrated emphasis on ethnic specificities and religious orthodoxies that has made it more opportune for some groups to lobby for resources on ethnic-specific interests, rather than on the basis of the shared experience of racism. The very real cultural and religious differences between people of Asian and African descent have therefore become translated into bureaucratic practice and political lobbying. This is ironic since growing numbers of all these communities are 'home-grown,' i.e., born and educated in Britain, and it is racism (whether there is cultural difference or not) that continues to ensure that Black people's access to resources and services is circumscribed.

That I lived in racist Britain for most of my life has shaped my subjectivity. Whether I live in Canada or in England, racism continues to affect me. Here in Canada, having lived under colonialism, I identify with and give solidarity and support to the struggles of the First Nations peoples for their autonomy and self-government. Thus, to identify myself as Black living in a non-Black world is to bring it home. Racism, sexism, classism, and the power relations that structure all areas of life are what I live and struggle with every day. The oppression that exists in our society I know not only theoretically. I live it every day.

I tend to agree with Gemma Tang Nain (1991), that Blackness has been accepted by those not of African descent as a result of their experience of racism in Britain. But that is not to say that the term means the same to them as it does for persons of African descent. I am conscious that I speak from a position of choice; for those of African descent, living within a dominant non-Black culture that sees Black people in disparaging, stereotyped ways, that choice is absent. In a discussion of the ambiguity surrounding the question of who is "Black,"

Gemma Tang Nain (1991) questions the viability of Black feminism and suggests
the adoption of anti-racist/socialist feminism. Thus, "White-ethnic" women who
share some of the same struggles as Blacks with respect to racism would not be
excluded from the term "Black." I think that while that might be appropriate for
describing a particular philosophy of feminism, it is cumbersome for describing
identity and social location. My use of Black and non-Black is deliberate to
provoke us into thinking about institutional practices, such as racism, that are
socially constructed to divide us from one another and me from myself. I am
perhaps making a circular argument here, because the various terms, Chinese,
Japanese, Indian, Pakistani, etc., reveal distinct social identities that cannot be
lumped together under the term Black, Brown, or woman of colour. Thus, in
some contexts, arguably, it is important to reveal the historicity of the subject,
multiple social identities and their location in our everyday practices.

Jenny Bourne (1987), in a rigorous critique of identity politics and Jewish
feminism, argues that identity politics are the product of a feminism that is sep-
aratist, individualistic and inward-looking, a feminism that personalises racism
rather than seeing it primarily as a structural and institutional issue. I support her
critique and her perspective on racism, but I am discomforted as well. Although
she supports the personal as political, she ends her argument by splitting the
personal from the political, thus disregarding of how individual subjectivities are
constituted and lived.

The question is: how can we build resistance and commitment in a society
where the social institutions and organisations encourage us to consider social
issues and concepts as if we were on the outside, detached from the very relationships and practices that produce them? The problems faced by some are
seen as individual rather collective problems. How can we get people to see that
we need communities of resistance and a commitment to a politics of hope if we
are to effect change? It is only when we stop splitting the private from the public and political world and recognise that politics are not confined to public,
organised spheres of practice that we will be in a position to transform the
world. Every action we take, every word that we utter, is political: it relates to
someone's politics somewhere. Furthermore, to think of some things as political
and others as not is to support dualistic and hierarchical thinking and being.

Identity politics are far from simple. They point to the need for dialogue,
for ways for us to learn from each other. Dominant non-Black culture has not

legitimated my difference; rather, I have come to see myself as an outsider, alien-
ated from others. I feel both hurt and anger that we are divided from each other
at every turn, that our collective resistance is always being undermined rather
than strengthened. Today, while many women are, I think, conscious of sexism,
they are not conscious of discrimination based on race, class or sexuality. It is
important for me, as an woman who has lived on the periphery, to reflect critically on the constitution of my subjectivity in a racist, non-Black society, which
(at worst) defines itself as multicultural. I think that the feminist practices of
naming, deconstructing, reconstructing and reframing cannot be separated from
the lives we live or the institutions in which we work. We must, I think, fully
grasp that knowledge is socially organised, that the world is socially constructed and hence changeable. I have a vision of a different world and I intend to
continue to struggle until it is realised.

## Melody Sylvestre

From the age of five to sixteen I lived in a primarily White suburb northwest of
Toronto and I identified with the dominant culture. The only time I recognised
myself as being different was when I looked in the mirror. During my childhood,
I never questioned why I could not attend neighbourhood picnics. I thought I was
ostracised because of something personal, not because of the colour of my skin.

When I was sixteen years old our White suburb was rapidly evolving into a
dynamic multicultural community. A Black population was growing. But violence was growing too; gang conflicts between young Black and White youth
were taking place in shopping malls and on school playgrounds.

When, as an adolescent, I began to form relationships with individuals of
different cultural backgrounds and skin colours, I met resistance from my
boyfriends' families. I was considered either too light or too dark, not Black
enough for those who were Black and too Black for those who were White. My
first love was a man of Jamaican descent, born in Britain. I recall distinctly being
referred to by his mother as a "coolie," a term coined by the British imperialists
to denote a servant or a peasant.

Once when he and I were leaving Sparkles, a teen disco in the CN Tower
in Toronto, we had to walk through a crowd of Black youth. I recall the women
hissing at me because he and I were together. Throughout that relationship I was
made to feel like an outsider because I was not Black. Meanwhile, my parents

cautioned me against a future relationship with someone of a different racial background.

I felt the same sense of difference throughout university, never quite being accepted in either the Caribbean or African associations. A few of my friends belonged to those groups, but the majority of my friendships were with Whites. However, I longed to investigate Black cultures.

As my life progressed, I became involved with men from various cultures: Nigerian, Jamaican, French-Canadian, German-Canadian and, eventually, the father of my child, a man of Ukrainian descent. While I was pregnant I began to encounter blatant racism for the first time. My partner did not anticipate his family's harsh reaction to our relationship. He was miffed. His mother had raised him to believe in equality. But, like so many others, she had never expected him to act on it as he had.

After our child was born he was examined for his degree of Whiteness. The persecution of my son and me continued. For example, during one Thanksgiving dinner at my partner's family's home, the toast was: "It should be as it is in the old country, that people should marry those of the same nationality." Even a complete stranger told me my child would be perfect if only he had blue eyes instead of brown.

During my university years, I was constantly asked where I was from. After I named the Toronto suburb that my family lived in, the questions would continue: "No, where are you really from?" People would look inquisitively at my son and me; a dark-skinned woman and a blond, fair-skinned child seemed strange to them. Some would ask if he was really my son or if his father was White. I wanted to say, "More than likely, somewhere in this city, there's a White woman walking around with a Brown baby."

The relationship with my partner has proved difficult. I know that some of it has to do with his own struggles — being pulled in different directions, having to decide between holidays with his own family and the holiday we had planned, trying to please a family that would never accept his choice of a partner, a family that believed that I would only hinder his advancement.

We eventually moved to the East coast, to a small town with a predominantly White population. A neighbour quickly told me that when my son entered school, he would be called "half-breed." It was obvious that I was "from away." There was absolutely no way of blending into the community. I learned that some people would automatically make assumptions about my values and traditions, would assume that I had a non-Christian philosophy and would ask strange questions like, "What do you eat at Christmas?"

Upon returning to Toronto recently, I was stunned by the number of inter-racial and bi-racial children. I felt confident and secure, for myself and for my child. I assumed that we had entered an atmosphere of racial harmony. That illusion was short-lived. I soon realised that racism still exists here but in ordi-nary everyday exchanges. It is subtle, almost hidden. Today, in my work as a welfare visitor for Metro Social Services, I experience firsthand frustration and intolerance from people of all colours. I have been called a racist by White people, by Black people and by people who think I should be helping them since we are from the "same" part of the world. Several times, I have had inter-views with clients where not the slightest inkling of prejudice was apparent. Subsequent interviews with me or with other workers made it evident that these same, "nice" people were intolerant of me, other workers or other welfare recip-ients. Welfare workers can be hesitant to serve people from the same racial or background as themselves precisely because those clients may expect prefer-ential treatment.

When I tell others about my experiences with racism, most people still refuse to believe that racism is prevalent in Canadian society. One friend stated, "I've never noticed any racism. It's never affected me." For her, it does not exist. Similarly, on the subject of feminism, another friend said, "I've always been able to get whatever I wanted. Equality has never been an issue in my life." Despite those responses, my experience has forced me to examine closely the events, actions and reactions of those I come in contact with. The process by which I have come to understand the effects of racism has been personal; it has meant acknowledging my difference, struggling for a decade to fit in some-where, anywhere, accepting who I am, questioning whether I am Anglo-Indian or Canadian.

Even this society's emphasis on physical features reinforces how we see our-selves and each other. I think that as women, as visible minorities, we feel insecurity and fear in our daily lives. Discussions of racism, of feminism and of equality are considered taboo. We need to fight for equality in order to change our society from being unaccepting to accepting. By openly discussing different identities and values, by emphasizing the richness of the two cultures of my son's ancestry and by helping my son to confront questions about his ethnic identity, I hope to encourage a sense of confidence in him. The challenge facing our society is, I think, to find a way to promote pride and a sense of belonging as individuals and groups both create new identities and maintain aspects of their heritage. I intend to give my son the courage and confidence to determine his own identity in a positive way.

I am still searching for those who are like me, not so much in colour but in experience and understanding. I do not fit any nice, neat category, but rather am just present in Canadian society. Because I am present, I would appreciate it if the phrase "equal opportunity" were to have more than just mythical value. I may never be able to change the stereotypes, but I think that we can learn much by critically reflecting on our experience.

Ultimately, I want to hope that we can achieve social change through personal resistance and struggle. Beneath the skin, regardless of colour, we are all alive, and I think that we all deserve to feel the beauty and joy of living, sharing and respecting each other for who we are.

# REFERENCES

Jenny Bourne. *Jewish Feminism and Identity Politics* in **Race and Class**, Vol. XXIX, 1987, pp. 1-24.

Anne-Louise Brookes. *Teaching, Marginality and Voice: A Critical Pedagogy Not Critical Enough?* in **Canadian Perspectives on Critical Pedagogy, Canadian Critical Pedagogy Network Occasional Monograph**. No. 1, pp. 25-34 (Henley, D., and Young, J., eds., Winnipeg: Manitoba Press. 1990).

Amina Mama. *The Hidden Struggle: Statutory and Voluntary Sector Responses to Violence Against Black Women in the Home*, for the London Race and Housing Research Unit (Nottingham: Russell Press, 1989).

Gemma Tang Nain. *Black Women, Sexism and Racism: Black or Antiracist Feminism?* in the **Feminist Review**, No. 37, 1991, pp. 1-22.

Kathleen Rockhill. *The Chaos of Subjectivity in the Ordered Halls of Academe* in **Canadian Woman Studies**, Vol. 8, No. 4, 1987, pp. 12-17.

K. Victor Ujimoto. *Multiculturalism, Ethnic identity, and Inequality* in **Social Issues and Contradictions in Canadian Society**, B. Singh Bolaria, ed. (Toronto: Harcourt Brace Jovanovich, 1981).

## Janice McCurdy Banigan
# Backa Town*

**WHEN** I was nine years old, I took part in my first civil rights demonstration — a revolt in music class. The details are fuzzy after all this time, but I recall the most important ones like the exact desk where I sat when we finally put our plan into action.

We liked our music teacher, Mrs. Pierce, even though she had a rather subdued personality. She always seemed slightly out of touch with what was happening around her. Mrs. Pierce wasn't like most of my other teachers, who were downright racist. They had subjected us to all forms of humiliation. Despite that, and perhaps because we did not fully understand how racism works, we still tried to compensate for and measure up to the standards of those people. At age nine, the trait was fully developed in me. I felt it necessary to out-perform in order to achieve some acceptance. Our demonstration was the first time that I deviated from that. Poor Mrs. Pierce was in the wrong place at the wrong time. But it was her naïveté about things like racism which put her there.

We had small, black-coloured books which we used in music class. They were dog-eared from the countless small hands that had handled them over the years. Among the songs in them was an assortment of Stephen Foster's music, such as "Old Black Joe" and "Down by the Swanee River." Whenever we sang them, I'd always feel embarrassed and ashamed. The shame made me the angriest. Singing words like "nigger" and "piccaninny" always made me feel as though I'd been slapped in the face. Some of the other children taunted us, knowing that we hated the songs. When Mrs. Pierce played the piano, her back to us, she was totally oblivious to the cruel titters and pointing fingers. If we reacted, we would be the ones to get in trouble.

I don't remember who the ringleader was, but one day, after a heated discussion, all the Black kids united. We decided not to sing any more insulting songs about Black people. We unanimously decided on "Old Black Joe" as the being the most offensive. The lyrics depicted Joe as an ignorant child, unaware of the realities of slavery. To demonstrate our feelings, we tore out one of the pages. I felt elated and free as I ripped the page from the book. Ordinarily, I would have considered such an act as wrong. I had been taught that books should be treated with great respect, but this time the end justified the means.

By arrangement, we all sat together. After we tore out our pages and then explained our actions, we could see that Mrs. Pierce was struggling to understand what was happening. She didn't recognise the racism inherent in the lyrics, but she was compassionate and didn't punish us. And we didn't sing any more of Foster's songs. Sadly, though, I don't think she ever really understood why we found them so offensive.

*An excerpt from an upcoming novel.

**Carol Talbot**

# Soul Sounds

The drums beat the rhythms of our soul
   and we  hear them
       hear them
       hear them

The drums beat the rhythms of our soul
   and we  hear them
       hear them
       speak to us
       speak to us
       speak soul
        to us
        to us
        to us
         us
         us

In our deep within we hear hear
In our deep within we hear hear
Our mothers grandmother mother
   mothers grandmothers mothers
     speaking speaking
     soul soul song
     soul soul song

Dark hands beating rhythms
    strong hands
    gentle hands
    heart hands
   beating rhythms

soul rhythms
soul rhythms
 deep
 deep

Voices of the ancestors they
Voices of the ancestors shimmering through
 generations
  upon
 generations

We come to hear
 to speak
 our rhythms
 to make our voices heard
Over the white waters of wisdom
Under the currents of domination
We will be heard
And we will listen

Drumbeats of our fathers
Drumbeats of our mothers
We hear you
And listen to your call

Their goddess does not wear our face
her hair is not our hair
Her skin not ours either
Their herbs are not of our land
Their legends or their stories

Our forefathers and mothers
have walked this land
For four hundreds of years

In their footsteps
 singing their songs
 worshipping their gods
 lost in their metaphors

We are children of disinheritance
 lost on a sea of illusions

Mirrors reflect not ourselves
      only shadows of selves past
      and distorted images of their present

These are hard words
      to speak to them of their understandings
      to come out of hiding with some of our pain
      and explain their oppression to them
      only to be misunderstood and abused again

We must trust ourselves in our search
      allow ourselves the emotional spiritual space
      they seek for themselves
We must be patient with our     ambivalences
                             confusions
                             angers
                             pain

We know their mirrors are not all true
And the reflection of themselves is marred
We each must travel our own roads to self knowledge
Let us honour the journey ...

*I am*
   *alone.*

*The anger*
   *that flows from this reality*
   *is overwhelming*

~ Untitled

## Isolation

**Lisa Valencia-Svensson**

# Untitled

The fragmentation
     is so overpowering.
I am alone in a white world
And the barriers
     that divide me
     from other women of colour
     are immense.

Trying to undo the frame of reference
     exhausts me.
Wanting
     so badly
          to reach out
          to touch them
          to say I know.

The obstacles
     reduce me
     to my very barest,

I am alone.
     I am alone
In a tangible, real community
     I am
          alone.

The anger
     that flows from this reality
          is overwhelming.

### Lisa Valencia-Svensson
# Untitled

In the middle
of the black white issue
Placed in the hazy zone
of racial irreconcilable
Culture sweeps around me
in a wash of foreignness
Permanently marking my thoughts
Shaping my history
Filling my needs

The divides that put me further from
        those around me come near
So few faces to validate my own
The realities of the multicultural metropolis
Finally hitting home.

**Josee Brome**

# Untitled

what do i do with my unresolved anger
Screaming is socially unacceptable,
murder a bad idea.

i liberate my soul, someone is always
trying to resurrect Uncle Tom.

what do i do with my lost love
misplacing myself in order to understand
has not helped me.
Screaming is socially unacceptable,
murder a bad idea.

my politeness in social situations is
merely part of my humanity, it's
time to stop taking it for granted.

How many times am i going to have to
say it?

### Camille Isaacs
# Neither/Nor

Autumn leaves flutter
like applause at a polite recital
stiff-necked soldiers march in formation
poppied wreaths placed staidly in tribute
spectators pause, bow their heads
a moment of eerie silence
cannon shot reverberates
through the hole in my stomach

3 Black men approach
draped in chains and carrying banners, beating drums
chanting, "Rem'ber the Inhumanity
of Slavery and Neo-Slavery!"
handing out fliers
        the language of the unheard
forcing confrontation

I know my forefathers weren't kilt-wearing, bagpipe-playing
        ruddy-faced soldiers
**that is not my history**
mine were the ones in the chains
yet Canadian-born
**this is my history**

I walk away from both
neither changing nor memorializing

*When I came to this land*
*I was fed another tongue*
*and, bit by bit,*
*it filled my mouth*
*until I could not speak*

~ MOTHER TONGUE

# FIVE

# Language & Identity

**Susan Lee**

# Mother Tongue

My tongue was given to me by my mother
in the land of the Other
with this tongue
sounds, words, and meanings
were given and exchanged
My tongue,
freely floated, darted and
created
centred in my mouth
it created an ability
to be heard

When I came to this land
I was fed another tongue
and, bit by bit,
it filled my mouth
until I could not speak
I was forced to swallow
My mother tongue
to form new words
in order to be heard

My mother's tongue
swallowed, digested and
expelled
almost forgotten except
for the taste which lingers in my mouth

**Camille Hernandez-Ramdwar**

# The Creation of Identity: Challenges for Women of Colour Writers Living in the West

THE struggle to create or to maintain an identity has been a complex one for women of colour living in the West. Much of our work, our creativity, is fraught with it. On the frontier of the written word, voice, appropriation, colonial language and access have been at the forefront. We can only write from our own perspectives. We can imitate other points of view, but we will always be revealing our own vision. Whose gaze is that? As women of colour, we are situated in a world that demeans us, that attempts to silence us, that tries to define us. Are we capable of resisting through affirming an identity that arises from within us?

Himani Bannerji offers one perspective on the subject in her essay, *The Sound Barrier*:

> We are other than a binary arrangement of identities, even though negatively or inadvertently we are caught in a racist-imperialist definition — its ideological and institutional practices. The overwhelming preoccupation with what "they say we are" and "what we are not," our "theorisation" by "them" precludes much exploration or importance of who we actually **are**.

How can we break out of reaction as a response? As women of colour, we are situated in a White supremacist patriarchy. How can we express ourselves beyond that reality? For me, writing is often catharsis, an outlet for the pressures of living in Canadian society. However, I have heard criticism that such writing is "confessional," i.e., not "real" writing, not "universal" or "transcendent." I wonder if there is writing by women of colour that is not confessional. What purpose is there in abstracting ourselves, in writing about lives we don't lead, about situations we will never find ourselves in? Does it also mean that we can emote, that we merely react to the injustices we face daily as we continue the struggle that we and our ancestors have undergone for hundreds of years? Ntozake Shange has a poem that argues:

> we deal wit emotion too much
> so why don't we go on ahead & be white then/
> & make everythin dry & abstract wit no rhythm & no
> feeling for sheer sensual pleasure/yes let's go on & be
> white/we're right in the middle of it/ no use holdin
> out/holdin onto ourselves/ let's think our way outta
> feelin/

In Shange's poem, being "coloured" connotes feeling, expression, emotion. It is set in opposition to Whiteness, the preserve of abstract linear thought and rationality. Are we seeing a woman of colour who has internalised dominant notions about us as a group? Or is Shange asserting the right to express her reality as a woman of colour in America?

Toni Morrison's *Playing in the Dark* describes the construction of an Africanist presence in the White literary imagination. She takes as given that this presence has infiltrated our collective conscious and states that much has been postulated about Black reaction to the Africanist presence. But how do we move beyond it? If the White literary imagination is imbued with an Africanist presence and, therefore, it is in the mainstream media, common images, the school curricula, etc., then how do we  move beyond reacting once again to the norm?

It is important to note that Bannerji and Morrison are coming from dissimilar experiences. Bannerji, coming from a Bengali experience and culture where her self and self-worth were represented in certain ways, recognises the loss of what could have been more profoundly than Morrison does. Morrison, an African-American woman, has been denied true representation of herself and her multiple realities in mainstream American culture. Those of us who have lived a North American, Western colonised experience may not be as aware of what might have been or what could be as are people of colour who live in non-White, post-colonial societies. Our realities have been constructed for us from birth. Much of our energy and creativity is put into resisting that construction. This isn't to say that there can be no revolution, but the form our revolution will take must be different from that of our sisters in other parts of the world.

When Audre Lorde says, "The master's tools will never dismantle the master's house," we can recognise her awareness of her subject position. Lorde was an African-Caribbean-American lesbian. Although she lived most of her life in the United States, she came to recognise the limitations of the "tools" given to her. Lorde was able to move within the confines of American society, to lay claim to and maintain her own voice.

Similarly, Cherrie Moraga, a Chicana lesbian, is particularly aware of the limits of language and searches for a truly expressive voice. Moraga moves between English and a variety of Spanish styles, but all are insufficient for her. She longs for a **mestiza** language and culture, one that is organic, that springs from its own source and validates itself. She, like Lorde, is set the task of constantly having to define and redefine herself in a society that wishes to silence her.

Let me make it clear that I do not wish to set up a binary opposition where, on the one hand, women of colour in the West and "Third World" women (i.e., the Bengali woman in India, the Ainu woman in Japan, or the Yoruban woman in Nigeria) do not have to struggle with issues of identity and voice and, on the other, those of us living in White-dominated societies and cultures do have to struggle with them. It is much more complex than that. We must take into account state policies of ethno-centricism, patriarchy, classism, heterosexism, migration, exile and neo-colonialism.

I would argue, however, that there is a difference in the way we approach an identification of self. At a recent gathering, I heard Bannerji speak about her introduction to the notion of race and how strange and peculiar it felt to have to define herself in those terms. I marvelled at how liberating it must be to never have had to think about such a category. But I also had to question what categories Bannerji was familiar with in India (i.e., caste, class, ethnicity). Bannerji's notion of self, of identity, was only really challenged when she immigrated to England and then to Canada. Confronted with a White supremacist system, all her notions of who she was in India (in terms of ethnicity, class, gender) disappeared. She had become a "paki," "South Asian" or "East Indian." None of those labels are her choice, none of them make any sense to her. She maintains her notion of who she is and where she comes from. Most of us who were born or raised here or in other White-dominated countries have no such compass.

One tactic employed by women of colour in the West who are searching for a more self-defined identity has been to name themselves in terms of their pre-colonial, ancestral origins. In an effort to retain some notion of difference within difference (i.e., a more suitable identity than the all-encompassing and generic "women of colour"), some women have opted for more essentialist categories, such as African, First Nations, etc. But a return to definitions based on historical origins means that centuries of history in the West — the realities of colonialism, imperialism, migration, miscegenation, acculturation and geno-cide — are denied. Individual differences, such as sexual orientation and class are also denied.

It is perhaps an extreme reaction to revert to a "glorious past" when it denies a more pressing reality: we cannot return to an untangled and "pure" cultural or "racial" past, and as the descendants of survivors, we are very different from our predecessors. We are more than our ancestors who first encountered or who were forcibly brought here by Europeans. With the exception of First Nations peoples, we are also vastly different from the people who now inhabit the areas of our forbears. One attempt to explain this cultural hybridity is the use of hyphenations, i.e., African-Canadian, Chinese-American, etc. But can these limiting definitions, these labels, even begin to tell our stories?

In some of the writing by women of colour we are, perhaps, beginning to move away from a preoccupation with labelling and towards defining identity through various forms of expression and storytelling. However, in North America, women of colour are constantly having to react to racism. That fact invades our writing and other forms of creative expression. We are involved in struggle and, through it, resistance. If we are to move beyond resistance, we must be careful not to fall into traps that will weaken our defense. Division on the basis of ancestral origin may feel comfortable to those of us who can claim a single origin, but how useful is it in the here and now? How much do the politics of division further separate us, further pit us against one another? Although women of colour are not a homogenous group, I think that divisions along the lines of political commitment and investment in the struggle would be more useful than "racial" divisions (which were, after all, invented to control us). It is a testament to the power of the construction "race" that it continues to keep us fighting amongst each other.

As women and men of colour, it is my fervent hope that we find our voices and develop some sense of self through creative and political expression and that the need for outdated labels and fictitious racial categories diminishes.

### Ayanna Black

# Inglish: Writing with an Accent

TAHAR Ben Jelloun writes, "the act of speaking is perhaps illusionary because it occurs in the language of the Other ... "For me, this word "Inglish" is far from being an illusion: it is a reality, it is our construct. We have spoken, and we have spoken within an important context! That's an important act. I cannot think of anyone who articulates it better than Jelloun when he says "What is most important ... is not what the mother said, but the fact that she spoke."

As a writer of African descent, I asked myself, what does it mean: writing with an accent? Is it writing out of an ancestral tradition that is central to speech? A synthesis of the oral, the literary and the visual? In Ghana, for example, symbols are painted on cloth, representing Ghanian proverbs, sayings and myths. Is this writing with an accent to be considered post-modern or post-colonial writing?

For the past five hundred years, books have been written to glorify European culture and many of these are written from a patriarchal and imperialist perspective. That approach continues to flourish, particularly in institutions and among some writers and scholars. Euro-centrism persists in the "intellectualism" of even the more progressive thinkers. This is the kind of structural and institutional impediment that I must break down in order to create a space for my work. Historically, my ancestors did not sit and wait for institutions to bring about change. People of African descent have had to forge new pathways for themselves; before dub poetry became popular, it was not accepted in mainstream literary tradition but was viewed as a fringe phenomenon.

I have come to realise that I have to use the vernacular in the manner that I see fit and that the English language falls into that terrain. The English language is not my enemy. I have the power to use it to my advantage, as did my ancestors, for survival and flexibility. I think that one of the strong points of the British is their understanding of the power of culture and language. In Paula Burnett's introduction to the *Penguin Book of Caribbean Verse*, she reminds us of those British characteristics when she writes "The British never made the mistake of underestimating the importance of language." Upon the arrival of slaves from Africa, they separated those who spoke the same language to prevent rebellion.

As an African-Canadian writer, I am drawing from a painful and complex history of slavery and colonisation and the dispersal of Africans to various parts of what is termed the New World. But in spite of that exploitation and brutality, we have managed to overcome tremendous obstacles in order to create a synthesis of ancient African literary traditions and imperialist literary constructs. Thus, Jamaican Creole is a dynamic marriage of English and African languages. Louise Bennett's poetry is an excellent example of this. What follows is the last stanza from her poem, *Colonisation in Reverse*:

> Wat a devilment a Englan!
> Dem face war an brave de worse,
> But me wonderin how dem gwine stan
> Colonizin in reverse.

This poetry is relevant to those engaged in what Burnett describes as a "search for forms of creative cohabitation" forms that allow for "the assertion of cultural self without the denial of that assertion to others, and the sharing of as much as can be shared."

Jamaican Creole was not taught nor was its use encouraged in my school days. It was not spoken by me or my peers. Yet even though it was viewed as an inferior language, I was very interested in it and found my life illuminated when it was spoken, especially during the times I went to pantomime.

But I will admit that it wasn't until 1985 that I penned my first poem in Jamaican Creole. It wasn't a very easy poem to write. Indeed, I was apprehensive. I wasn't sure that I could translate the music, the rhythm, with vigour and meaning and maintain the strong voice that I was hearing and feeling. Writing it opened an important path for me as a writer. I was no longer a silent listener, an observer, of that language. I was now an active speaker.

# REFERENCES

Bennett, Louise. *Colonisation in Reverse* in **The Penguin Book of Caribbean Verse** in English. Paula Burnett, ed. (New York: Penguin, 1986), pp. 32-33.

Burnett, Paula. *Introduction* to **The Penguin Book of Caribbean Verse**, pp. xxii-xxiv.

Jelloun, Tahar Ben. Harrouda. Cited in Elizabeth Mudimbe-Boyi's *Travel, Representation and Difference, or How Can One be a Parisian* in **Research in African Literature**, Vol. 23, No. 3,1992, pp. 25-39.

Joanne Arnott

# Swallowed/Whole:
# Down the Path of Assimilation

**FROM** what I've read and from what I've heard around me, there are a lot of people, women especially, who are mad at the English language. I am not. It is my language and it links me to people like myself all over the world. The English language, in spite of all the travesty and cruelty that has gone on and does go on in and for this language, is also a gift. There must be five, ten or one hundred times as many of non-Anglo English speakers as there are indigenous ones. Let our voices be raised.

Two of my four grandparents, from what I understand, spoke English as a second language. My mother's mother, born in what later the same year became Saskatchewan, was French and French-Belgian. Her family, the nuns and the priests who took an equal hand in raising her, and her community were all Francophone. At age twenty-seven, she married my grandfather, an English speaker of European descent who was born in Nova Scotia. Their children were raised speaking English.

My fathers' father was born and raised in Manitoba in a Scottish, Gaelic-speaking household in an English-speaking community. He married my grand-mother, who had migrated from Ontario with her mother and siblings and who spoke English. That grandmother, who like her husband died the year my father turned twenty-one, was said to be Irish. However, I have since discovered that she was Irish and Native Canadian.

When I was growing up my mother taught us a litany of the heritages we shared: French, Belgian, Scottish and Irish. There were two notable absences: Native (Six Nations) and British. I remember challenging my mother about excluding the British; we do speak English after all. She made it clear to me that the British were the colonisers and that we were not them. A long time later, my challenging of the absence of my Native heritage brought no easy answers. Because of that denial, the importance of my Native heritage is greater than that of my European heritage.

I am daughter to the Six Nations, yet were I to find them, I could not speak to any of the traditional elders in the language that cradles the culture. Though I might listen, I could not hear what they had to teach and only the rhythms might be more or less familiar. I would be restricted to the non-verbal aspects: looking, seeing, feeling. All is not lost, however. Given the depth and breadth of cultural domination, there is an excellent chance that in every Six Nations community I could find present-day elders who speak English.

There are, however, certain tendencies of the English language that need to be countered, hazards that are not necessarily found in other languages. For instance, English has the concepts of mind/body spirit, private property and linear causality in its very fibre. When I think about that I feel sad. I long for a language to teach my children that would not bind them to those concepts. My children are very important to me, and I yearn for a language that would have them be not mine but part of a community of people.

Both my parents were raised as English speakers, so were the parents of my partner and so were we. This legacy makes our children third-generation English speakers, and it is time for a certain amount of acceptance of that fact and comfort with that language.

Through the English language I can say what I want to most everyone. We understand each other and, from time to time, we are thrilled by the beauty that comes out of our mouths when English becomes the conduit for expressing our deepest and fullest selves, our wildest creativity and our wisest knowing. Through knowing English, I have listened to the experiences of women and men all over the world — people geographically dispersed, culturally diverse and far-flung by the passage of time.

In my own family English is the crossroads — the point where several cultures meet.

Is this good?

Are you kidding?

Who would trade culture, language, or history that could be passed on from one generation to another for the ability to listen and speak of the depth and breadth of racist and colonialist oppression all over the world? It isn't a choice that we are afforded or one that is even practical, given the world we live in today. What we do have in a dominant language, although colonial and charac-terised by an exploitive past, is access to the experiences of other people. Given that, I am glad that I have English at least, if the alternative is silence.

Throughout the world, each of us has a context, history and depth; we have feelings and sensations, perceptions of the life around us. We can balance the hazards of the English language and the history of the world and our place in it. We can be mindful of this as we nurture our young, as they nurture their own, and so on, until we fade away as the stream of life flows on.

Let the stories be told in whatever languages are heard. Let the songs be sung.

6
SIX

# Finding "Home"

**Karen Shadd-Evelyn**

# Mother Africa: A Drum Song for Scattered Harvests

I hear my Mother calling
in the rhythm of the drum, beating:

"Come home ... child ... come.
Your sister cries;
Your brother waits,
And hates the tribe that took you hence.
Your father died, from mourning you;
warriors — gone, to beat the trees,
near empty village bowed down to its knees:
      an easy prey.

Your Caribbean cousins laugh
      and weep, in raucous bray,
filling in the spaces where you were,
their carefree gazes sweep
the island shores for signs of you
or others, who might bring news
to their mothers, taken from
this shore a thousand lives before.

I weep for you, child, those of us who stayed
Remember how we played the drum
And danced when harvest time was done.
      Do you dance now, where you have gone?
      We beat the drum to call you home.
      You never come."

I hear my Mother calling, calling in the drum.
I dance the harvest, but  it's been too long ...
      ... too long ago ...

No more my brother waits.
my sister's tears are dry;
they have forgotten how I danced, and say
that I abandoned them, and should accept my fate.'

The cousins, too, disowned, the kin
    all scattered in the wind, deny
       each other, pretend not to recognise we had one

Mother — weep no more
    We hear the drum
      the distance is too far ...
          ... we cannot come.

### Camille Hernandez-Ramdwar

# The Blood is Strong (A Bi-dialectical Existence)

**THERE** was a time in my life when I was confident I would "go home." "Home" was not my birthplace, nor the land where I grew up, but far away in the Caribbean, in the land of my dreams (literally), a home that spoke to me in spirit and blood. When I walked the earth of that home, my feet rooted, I felt part of the dust of ancestral bones that mixed with the land. I responded to the *bush bush* of spirit whisperings in the bamboo groves where waterfalls beckoned me. The ocean cleansed me. I would return to that land because I had no other place to call my home.

In my passport my place of birth is listed as Winnipeg, Canada. Strange how that document, which I use to return to my "dream" home, my spiritual and ancestral home, denies me a whole and complete identity. I am legally, technically, semi-culturally, "naturally" a Canadian, but for all the years I've been in Canada I have never once felt "at home." The connection, the electro-magnetic field, the early emotional pull that I am supposed to feel when walking where my navel string is buried is non-existent. I have always felt a stranger, in transit, as if I should be carrying another passport, as if someone had lied to me about my real birthplace, as if the stork screwed up. Ironically, I have a sister born in Trinidad, two years older than I, who is quite happy in this country. She feels no sense of loss or confusion about her identity. Why did fate land me right in the heart of (populated) Canada, where the Red and Assiniboine rivers meet First Nations' territory, Turtle Island, Muddy Waters?

Early on, I concentrated on returning to Trinidad, to righting the hand of fate, to settle the unsettled once and for all, packing my bags with a sense of finality. Like a tropical bird in captivity, I longed for the twelve-hour sun, the rainy season, the sea breeze and heat. I felt exposed, my camouflage useless in a monochromatic world of greys and whites.

Perhaps it was the idealism of youth. Perhaps I never realised how fully acculturated I am, despite my protestations to the contrary. Perhaps because I am responsible for two children now — and as a Cancer woman I am a highly protective mother — I have had to reconsider my exodus. It is not as simple as packing my bags and boarding a plane. I may not feel Canadian, but does that make me Trinidadian?

The other day, I played Black Stalin's song, "We Can Make It If We Try." Why would this song about the struggle of a nation (my nation?) against adversity bring tears to my eyes if I haven't lived in Trinidad? I haven't come close to dealing with the difficulties that people living there have endured:

> And our country facing its darkest hour
> And our people need us today more than ever
> But in our fight to recover
> If ever you feel to surrender
> It have one little thing that I want you always remember:
> We can make it if we try just a little harder
> If we just give one more try life would be much sweeter.

I listen to Black Stalin's song and cry because I wonder if I will ever "go home" to Trinidad, where times are harder than where I am now. If I stay in Canada I face other risks: losing my spirit, my sense of identity. How can I know who I am here without knowing where I come from? A Trini could die from cultural deprivation in this place, despite Caribana with it's safe and secure barricaded masqueraders. Caribana is a tease: it does not satisfy, it can break hearts and, for those who know, it can send yuh in a frenzy for de real ting.

To stay here means the constant day-to-day wearying experience of racism in its many guises. Trinidad is still suffering a neo-colonial hangover, but I don't believe that can compare with the threat of White supremacy that people of colour endure here. As the multicultural blend in Canada increases, so do the instances of racism. This isn't a new phenomenon: anti-Aboriginal violence has been going on for centuries.

White Canadians are my nemesis. It has taken me years to reach that conclusion and to say it. I am, after all, half-White, a child of an interracial relationship. As a mixed-race, Caribbean-Canadian woman, I have been forced to live in the White world. I have had White friends, loved (or tried to love) enough White men, sat through enough racist comments and jokes and excused enough White people for their ignorance. Now I want to retreat, to have minimal contact and, above all, not to trust. I may show my White family a bit more tolerance because I know what to expect of them, but the idea of spending the rest of my life in a country dominated by White people is an unsettling one.

With a foot in each culture, I straddle this hemisphere, longing for home — an exile in the land of my birth, a stranger in my native country. I am homesick for a place I have only visited. It has been years of struggle to name myself in Canada, to collect and then select from the labels that we all seem to need to survive here. In my case it is: mixed-race-woman-of-colour-Caribbean-Black-Asian-Aboriginal-Hispanic-Indo-Brown.

To leave this country would only mean I would have to undergo identifying myself again. I am a completely different person in Trinidad, where elements of post-colonial race, class and gender categories move in different spheres and according to another set of rules. It is unsettling to interact in a society where how I am perceived by others is surprising, even shocking. Although I may feel "at home" there, I know that I am not a native-born Trinidadian. Cultural misinterpretations constantly remind me that I am "from foreign."

I pack my bags once again, only for a visit. I imagine myself forever packing a bag, manoeuvring between Pearson and Piarco airports, living a double life, a bi-dialectical existence. During my last visit, I was actually challenged by a few Trinis: "How yuh mean "Canadian?" "Dis girl ent a Canadian! Yuh too lie! Like yuh gone Canada one week and come back an' now trying to tell meh yuh's a Canadian." I shake my head. How ah could feel so at home? How ah could jus' move so, learn anew what was robbed from me? How ah could tek root from de time de plane reach? An' looking up at de Northern Range, how dat view so familiar? How ah could understan kiskidee call? How come pan grab me and loose me? How jouvert is a long-forgotten story in meh veins retold and retold so ah could join the chorus? How ah could love yuh so? How every parting tear at meh breast, how ah huntin' down cascadoo soto never leave yuh? Every shape and crevice of the land — the north coast and mangrove swamp, cane fields and pitch, samaan tree and salt water, the zandolee and hummingbird, every note of kaiso and parang, tassa and chantwell and the beauty reflected on the faces of the people — all that is mine too. An' yuh tell meh ah romanticise it, honeymoonin an' love is bline. Ah say yes, but dat is all ah have for now. An' such unconditional love is a creative force in truth, ah cyan just leave it so. Ah comin' home! Ah mus come home again.

That sentiment I keep close to me, fiercely protective of what is mine. I believe it is my birthright, my inheritance. It keeps me going through minus-thirty degree weather, through seas of White and sometimes hostile faces, through racial straitjackets and police shootings, through the blood of my brothers and sisters that is spilled through White fear and anger. I hug that sentiment as close to me as I would a baby; it represents a beginning, hope and innocence. It keeps me going until I can return to Trinidad to recapture my true self. An' ah keep tellin meself, dis time when ah reach, ah playin' fuh keeps ...

**Silvana Hernando**

# Ten Thousand Kilometres Away

you are
getting on with your life

and
I
remember
the night
we didn't take our clothes off
because
we didn't need to,
how
we were dizzy with lust,
my hands
and tongue
learning new journeys
in our
unspoken native language

I recall
how
days later
when it was for sure
that we had fallen for each other
I was
     finally
          able to cry
because
I did not belong in your arms

You see
exile means

> a tied tongue
> more machines
> less pollution
> fewer hugs
> translation of myself

So
I went home
to untie my tongue
to pollute myself
to get my hugs
to not translate myself

Home had changed
       and so had I

I was amazed
at how much people touched each other

had I been away too long?
"This will always be your home,"
you said,
        your voice echoing on the line,
and
I know you meant it

I am no longer translating myself

Ten thousand kilometres away
you get on with your life
and I hold our promise
of a shared future.

**Brenda Joy Lem**

# Jung Ho's Daughter

I      In
a cool dark room
Auntie kneels
on the damp
earthen floor
hypnotised
staring into
schizophrenic light
candles
changing shadows
on brick walls
looming small
large retreating

A Buddhist drone
verses chanted
in fields
gongs
someone wailing
while
Auntie, stone-faced
recites bible scriptures
My mother, too young
to understand
shaking,
trying to wake
Grandma, from death

My mother
four years old
is learning
more than Chinese
is learning
on the run
Too terrified to move
lying rigid
her face hot
on the cool floor
bombs
searing the sky
black

Thirteen years, thirteen dialects

II    Dad says
"She oughta be ashamed
Born in Canada
been back

over thirty years
and can't speak English?"

Mom still cooks
while we eat
My brother makes
a joke
we all laugh
Mom says
"Nei gog mat yeh?"
We say
"Nothing"
Mom comes to the table
We finish eating in silence.

My sister,
"All American"
Dad would say
She, the pitcher
he, the coach
on the neighbourhood
softball team
I'd straggle
out to left field
skinny with braces
praying
the ball didn't
come my way.


III      I'm overseas
Hong Kong
learning Chinese
"Ni Hau ma? Wo hen hau.
Ching dzwo. Si si ni."
I sound like a
wind-up doll
to friends
who tell jokes
in Chinese
I say
"Nei gog mat yeh?"
They say
"Mo gwan see"
It was nothing
I am learning
more than Chinese.

In Hong Kong, I get
paid twice
the local
because I'm Canadian
but less than half

of a Brit
because I am Chinese
I read articles in the
South China Morning Post
patronizing, denigrating
the locals
A friend tells me not to
write any more angry
letters to the editor
I might end up with
concrete shoes in the
fragrant harbour.


IV    At last I am in China
I visit my family village
Nam Kai
Everyone meets me
for the first time
but they know me
from pictures
on the wall
They embrace me
"Jung Ho ga nui'
fun gay la!"

Ho's daughter
I kneel on the
earthen floor
shame
flushing my cheeks red
I lay my hot face
against the cool
terracotta
and
silently weep.

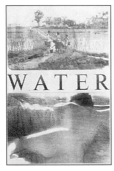 

These two mono prints were made by gum bichromate printing. It is a slow process, where depth and colour are added slowly in layers, through repeated soaking in pigments, exposure to light, long washes in water, drying and starting all over again. The process compliments my own slow journey as I found and created my identity through family history.

## Brenda Joy Lem

# Water Girl

**WATER** Girl is based on stories my mother told me about her childhood in China. As a young girl, her day in the village would start before dawn when she had to fetch the water supply for the day.

I have been making art for many years now. Only recently have I come to realise how much it is tied to understanding who I am, where I come from and how it is a form of resistance, a way of maintaining a cultural identity that is not dominant or recognised in North America. Along with that realisation, I have come to believe that some cultural traditions are embedded in us from our childhoods and that they will not disappear.

Like many Chinese-Canadians of my generation, I dreaded being Chinese: we considered any superficial symbol of Western culture to be cool, a way of escaping from our culture. Some of us became extremely proficient in Western writing, philosophy and the arts.

I believe that when we are stripped down to our own bodies, however, we cannot escape our personal, familial, cultural traditions. I believe there is strength in knowing that vast body of experience.

## Lisa Valencia-Svensson

# Tago*

Snatches of culture
Your islands painted across my mind
Like a billboard of lush tropical promises

Delicate morsels of fruit
Packed away in forbidding jars
I wear your lace your fibres
And dream of paradise

Philippines

    used to be a fantasy for me
    small parcels of land
    nestled off the coast
    surrounded by the blue, blue sea

Fih-lih-peenz

    syllables rolling off my tongue
    into the air and twisting round
    forming an invisible cloak of heritage
    I thought I wore so proud

Secrets scrawled across your wide face
your round cheeks nose mouth
The past looking out at me
Through your eyes

Why to this day do our realities remain
So tightly hidden in my heart?

* Tago is Tagalog for something hidden away.

## Alison Chan, Caroline Chan, Geoffrey Chan & Jennifer Chan

# Disappearing Trails: Reading Canada Writing Hong Kong

From this beach a lovely bit of road leads into Deep Bay and so home.

And if I were to enter this stretch of water and continue through it, across this sea would lie my home. But I stand here, facing the sea, my feet still rooted to this land. It seems enough for the moment to stand here and let my mind wander, to follow the drift and lull of the waves till they reach the other side, thudding lightly, lingering, then turning back to me.

THIS narrative is about memory, time and space, language, appearance and degrees of difference. It is about a journey that began in Hong Kong when the eldest of us was born and continues in Toronto with the birth of the youngest. Our arrival in Canada in 1980, at such young and formative ages, did not bring us to the journey's end, for even though we have spent just over half of our lives in Canada, Hong Kong has left an indelible imprint on us. Each of us has come to realise that Canada is not the final place for us, that our journey continues whether we like it or not. But, for now, we're stopping temporarily to look back at the old road, to see how much of it we can remember, for our story is really about what meaning Hong Kong — our former home, our former culture — holds in our anxious present (the anxiousness being rooted in our need to feel a sense of belonging in Canada). Though our individual journeys differ and we each speak from individual experience, there is as much commonality as there is dissonance. It's as if our cultural identities were determined by our dates of birth.

Our journey is specific and unique. Our "Chinese-Canadian" experience does not easily fit into the stereotyped mould of being "caught between two sets of values, traditions and lifestyles." Rather, our experience has taught us that there are no boundaries in the formation of cultural identities, no beginning and no end in the meeting of cultures. That meeting began in Hong Kong, long before we ever arrived in Canada.

The Chan-MacKenzie family's history embodies the cultural encounter upon which the farmer colony of Hong Kong was founded. Hong Kong's famous port symbolises the confluence of two cultures: Britain and China. Its colonial history carries the weight of generations of mixed families and mixed identities. That cultural confusion has trickled down to us. Our father's family is descended from several such encounters over a hundred years ago (one was between a Scottish sea merchant and a Chinese woman). It is this cultural ambiguity within the Chan family that is at the core of our current attempts to define our identity. Before we can go further, we need to retrace the past and find our footprints. In the following passages there are four voices.

~~~

Imagine a handful of handwritten postcards. The settings are where most of our memories of Hong Kong reside: our paternal grandparents' house (the Chans) in Killarney, Taipo Kau, and our maternal grandmother's house (the Poons) in Kotewall Road. Only now am I conscious of their significance as sites of cultural contention (East and West), as points between which our culturally-nomadic selves shifted from Sunday to Sunday as we alternated visits between our grandparents' homes. In between are intermittent snapshots of the landscape we grew up knowing as home, the countryside of Hong Kong. Faulty memory accords me only these snapshots.

> Winding roads spiral 'round the lush hills which
> roll up and down the countryside. The
> tropical greenery, as one climbs up, turns into
> open and bare rolling landscapes, the shrubs
> worn away by the wind and burning sun. I
> climb and climb (walk and walk on) until I
> reach the peak of the hill, which I know will
> look down onto the surrounding waters.

# 1979

Killarney, Taipo Kau. Where Papa's parents live and where English is the language of the house. I feel more comfortable here than at Kotewall Road. Here, there is the freedom of the countryside and the ease of transition between school life and here. Spoken English and British faces are the norm. During the week, we attend an English-speaking school, a melting pot of Eurasians, Americans and mostly British, the same faces we have as guests here at Killarney, a smouldering pot of mixed feelings and positions, of who or what is British or Chinese, of who looks British or Chinese. But I am left with a sense of freedom. I can belong neither here nor there but in-between, a mix of the two. At lunchtime, the family and guests all crowd around the day's offerings; my favourites are a chow mein dish with *tsa siu* (barbecued pork) and *lo bon tsai*, Chinese soup with black strands of seaweed. Things remind me faintly of being Chinese, but I put that at the back of my mind. I mostly feel my Englishness here; we know another language but somehow it doesn't fit. This is a haven. Time seems endless and I always feel safe and secure.

Kotewall Road. A massive colonial mansion, a relic of the past. It is our maternal grandmother's home, the matriarch of my mother's family (the Poons). The house always seems to be crowded with family when we visit. I have plenty of cousins to play with; we speak only Cantonese. This is where we get our Chineseness: the language, the customs, the food, the family. I am more aware of strictness and order. There is less land to explore than at Killarney, but the old stones and tiles of the mansion, the antique furniture, the framed portraits of ancestors that line the walls, reverberate with history and family tradition that is absent from Killarney; theirs is a family whose past is absent from the present. I can blend in here amongst the gaggle of relatives and amahs because I feel my place in the family. But I speak somewhat differently from my cousins because I go to an English-speaking school and speak both English and Cantonese at home. The other parts of ourselves, the other worlds my sisters and I inhabit, can't be shared with them because they wouldn't be able to understand our Englishness, the side that is gradually becoming the primary model for shaping our cultural identities.

> Crossing two borders, the borders between countries and the legacy of a mixed heritage, has heightened my sense of the ephemerality of place and belonging, of cultural identity. I exist

in places where you normally never look. One moment I am here, the next I have vanished, reappearing over there. It's uncontrollable.

# 1979

When I was ten years old and living in Hong Kong I had a great sense of the rate at which my body was growing. I noticed and anticipated the long, dull aches of my bones, and I noticed the tiny hairs on my arms which, when viewed at the right angle in the late afternoon sunlight, were a growing army of transparent white strands. Raising my arm and pointing it straight out towards the light, I could catch a glimpse of hairs I normally could not see and inspect their colour. I wondered if their colour would change as I grew. Perhaps they'd become a part of me and make me look different.

At the same time, I also wanted to fit in within my mother's family, where our Chinese identity was formed. At my maternal grandmother's house, I avoided those thoughts and thoughts of my English-speaking friends and school; they seem so distant and irrelevant.

My nose. A Chinese feature, small and flat against my face. From the time I was a child until my early teenage years it was a source of deep embarrassment for me. As a child, the sense I got from my father's family was to value things Western, especially looks, over things Chinese. I hated my nose. I couldn't bear the thought of people staring at my profile: the eyes not quite sunken in enough, the nose, flat and ugly on the face.

> This chinesement of her looks contains the best qualities of a
> chow mein dish. Succulent, fresh, kind-hearted and servile.
> The richness of the black hair adorning her head evokes
> strangely contrasting feelings in me. The same with the flat,
> angular features of her face (not unlike a monkey's). But the
> mysteriousness of her chinesely ways — the gentle bows of her
> head, the flash of her dark brown eyes — renders me flabbergasted.

Normally, I see myself as being White, not so much because I aspire to be White but because of being surrounded by fair-skinned people. It is when I consciously think about my appearance that I remember, with a jolt, that I look Asian. When I was younger, I used to wish that I could look like my White classmates and I felt somewhat unattractive beside them. Even now, vestiges of that sense of inferiority remain with me and, occasionally, I wonder what my girl-friends see in me besides my appearance. Sometimes I think I am more obsessed with racial difference than my friends and acquaintances.

> The chinesian aspect of my most permeable personality is a most helpful, hard-working little chap. Most days, this industri-ous little fellow with bold, black hair (hair black as night and reminding me of an oil slick) can be seen at the work site, deep in concentration on a piece of paper. This loyal worker will do almost anything one desires. Even dirty tasks usually left to the untouchables, this fellow will carry out in a spirit of thankful-ness and loyalty. One can almost certainly count on such a fellow to carry out all of one's needs. Almost every chinesian is of the same disposition: amiable, healthy, strong as a mule, and possessing the charm of a small, brown mouse.

~~

For almost thirteen years, I have tried to fit in, tried to be "invisible" in Canada. The way I live, my mannerisms and my friends are all testaments to my adop-tion of the Canadian way of life. Sometimes, I feel so steeped in Canadianisms and White, middle-class-led debates (the environment, feminism, post-mod-ernism, deconstructionism), that I wonder why I seem to be one of only a hand-ful of "visible minorities" engaged in such debates. When it comes to Chinese his-tory, customs or religions, I am as ignorant as a Western tourist in China, so when I visit Chinatown to shop or have a meal, I consciously have to try to fit in to that minority setting, my own minority, in order to be seen as one of the group.

~~

I was born in a hospital in Toronto. I am a Chinese-Canadian. All of my family, except me, were born in Hong Kong. I went there once when I was very little. In school many people have asked me what my origin is. When I tell them they sometimes say that I speak good English. In class I feel quite okay being Chinese. Some other Chinese people at school say it's strange because I wasn't born in China but in Toronto. They also think it's strange that I don't remember much Chinese. A friend once said that I wasn't keeping my culture when I didn't do a Chinese talent for my school's talent night. I also recall many people asking me to speak Chinese. I'm embarrassed to speak it. Sometimes I don't like being Chinese because of what people might think of me. I feel different because I don't look like other people and, by that, I mean mostly that I don't look White. At home, my mom sometimes speaks Chinese to my brothers and sisters. I don't like that much because I can't understand what she's saying.

I might want to change my surname to MacKenzie, my great-grandfather's surname. Maybe because it sounds non-Chinese. My dad's background is mixed, European and Asian. That's where MacKenzie comes from. Also, I would change my name to MacKenzie because it's original. I think it sounds kind of nice too. I think that "Jennifer Chan" sounds more suitable, though.

> I'll say that it was a smooth ride into the Canadian landscape. Assimilation took place. Mission successful.

~~~

# 1930

I was eleven then and just beginning classes at my new school in Toronto. I remember the taste, the nuances of each word that I spoke in my mind ...

| | |
|---|---|
| I'm | (The very definitive I. Uncharacteristic of me, rare that I should begin to tell myself to go out and accomplish something.) |
| Going | (Embarking to a new place, one where I felt I could fit in, slide in unnoticed.) |
| To | (A place or objective. Was it imaginary? Or the destination sure?) |
| Have | (A new possession in my hands, a tool I'll buy.) |
| A | (A singular object I desired.) |
| Canadian | (Something that belonged to this new country we came to.) |
| Accent. | (To speak! To stand up and sit down with.) |

I used to be very proud that my family spoke English without any trace of a Chinese accent and was rather scornful of people whose English was clumsily tainted with a foreign slant. Somehow, it gave me a feeling of superiority (a skill, strangely enough): we had mastered that aspect of White culture and therefore we fit into Canada better. At the same time, I had the uncomfortable sense of being a traitor to my race for considering it below me in that respect. After all, it was unnatural for Chinese to be speaking English in the first place. Perhaps it was born of envy of those who speak Cantonese fluently, which I do not. This dilemma about language has plagued me ever since we came to Canada.

In grade school, people asked me if I spoke "Hong Kongese." I never knew what to say, so I considered memorizing a set phrase for such situations.

The real story about Chinese School (Toronto): hated it, not interested in learning Chinese, was worst in the class, often faked illness to avoid going, didn't really understand what we read or wrote. Only too happy to quit at eleven years old, I wonder how I got through it at all.

My closest friends have never been Chinese, with one exception, and that was because she accepted me as an anglicised Chinese. The other "Oriental" girls I knew were, like her, directly from Hong Kong, but they seemed more interested in preserving Hong Kongness within their own tight circle than in knowing me.

Pure Canadian content: my friends, predominantly White, have told me that they have never thought of me as being a Chinese person. Finding that out made me feel numb. I suddenly sensed the power of assimilation; like an entopic wave, if not conscientiously resisted, it would overtake me.

~~~

As children, unaware of the complexities of adulthood, we saw things as they were. When we write about our Hong Kong experiences, our analyses are not the same as when we write about our Canadian ones; we are simply older and our perspectives have altered and widened. Time goes against our quest to connect with our memories, to find the place which has left us with an inaccessible store of knowledge.

> At present (and I date these thoughts because the journey has not ended), I face the near future with the haunt of Hong Kong over my shoulder. My roots, untouched for years, then severed just as they were taking hold, dangle and have grown a protective skin at their ends. Returning to Hong Kong at the age of eighteen, I had hoped to restore my severed memories, restore what had already disintegrated and blown away on the wind.

So when I go back — the second of us to return — the journey will take a different turn (perhaps as much as 180 degrees), towards the hills, towards the ocean once familiar to me. I go back hoping to restore fading photographs of my childhood, my home, to fill in the spaces where colour has lost its fullness. I go back hoping to till the hardened soil of thirteen years' absence, to dig up old roots, old secrets, that lie deep within the Chan family.

> I've been sent on a personal mission, you see,
> traversing the bridges of time and space.

## Lynette Harper with Mira

# Beyond the Beautiful Umbrella

I am the grandchild of Lebanese immigrants who arrived in Canada with dreams of wealth and adventure. Though neither of my grandparents received any formal education in this country, they learned well enough to become Canadian citizens and full participants in the social, economic, and political life of their community. As I read academic literature about migrant studies, cross-cultural adaptation and culture-learning in preparation for my study, the facts and figures and proposed theoretical frameworks overwhelmed me. The third person singular pronoun was invariably "he," even though innumerable studies suggest that men and women have fundamentally different experiences and perspectives. To learn about the actual experience of migration, I chose to do a life history which focused on one woman's problems and solutions, to exploring her own perspectives and interpretations of the transition.

I wanted to work with a Lebanese woman for many reasons. I already knew some people in Vancouver's Lebanese community, so I thought it would be easier to meet and work with someone who was part of it. My own Lebanese heritage has always intrigued me, and the study would provide a good opportunity for me to learn more about it. And I am deeply disturbed by the way modern mass media continue to stereotype Arabs as the "bad guys" and Arab women as passive, veiled victims. I hoped that my research would in someway correct such misrepresentations.

Our work began on a wet winter evening. Mira had made us each a cup of very strong Lebanese coffee, and I'd set up the tape deck, clipping a small mike to the sofa between us. Mira looked very calm and composed, while I felt nervous and edgy, fingering a pen and paper to make notes about our conversation, carefully searching for the right words with which to begin our work together.

## MIRA

I had a very, very happy childhood. We were very happy, I don't know whether I told you we are nine in the family. We grew up in a small village in Lebanon. I thought the whole world was there in my home town. I was not that anxious to go and learn about something else or know about anything else. I was so happy, I was the happiest, I was so spoiled. It was like a dream: everything a girl could wish to have in life, I had it. I had lots of friends and cousins, which is nice.

But there were a few things that I didn't like in our society, and I couldn't find an answer to why it's like that. There was no logical explanation to convince me that we should keep it. I always felt that there are a few things that we should throw away because we don't need it any more, especially when it comes to the relations between men and women. For example, why should I make my brother's bed? Why doesn't he? Why should I make him the breakfast? He has to make his own breakfast. These are little questions, but before, when I was twelve, thirteen, I never thought about it because this was the way we were brought up, I didn't know how to talk about it. But after that, when I was fifteen, sixteen, you start to wonder and ask why.

At that time I started to think on my own and analyze and wonder why is it like that. This was after I finished my grade thirteen in Lebanon. I went to Beirut, and it was my first trip outside my small world. And it was big. It was the first time in my life I stayed outside our house. I was in the residence. I used to come home every weekend. It was so hard for me. I found it very hard. I took pictures of my sisters, my brothers, my mom, and every time we missed them we put them on the bed in front of us and we cried, we wanted to go back. Plus, it was a totally different world, much bigger than where we grew up ...

## LYN

How long did you live in Beirut?

## MIRA

Well, unfortunately, because the civil war started, I couldn't stay. Just one year and we couldn't finish the whole year, the whole thing. It was very dangerous. Because we couldn't go back home. We couldn't go back. We were stuck for more than two months one time, no telephones, nothing, and our parents were so worried about us ... We had to stay in the shelters because at that time they started to slaughter people, just if you were either Moslem or Christian. That's how it started. It was very, very bad, so even though you were innocent, even though you are not affiliated or involved in any political organisations or anything, just because your last name is Christian or Moslem, they put an end to your life, and that's it.

It was horrible, this was the worst part of my life. And it stayed like that until I came in Canada! We lost every single thing. I couldn't bring the books or anything that I had in the university. We lost everything in our house and the house was blasted.

I wanted to fight everything that is causing death and destruction in my country. I thought that I'm the only one responsible, I should do something. All my friends left to different places in the world, and I stayed. They said, "Mira, why are you doing that? Why do you stay? Why don't you go?" I said no. I always believe that it's very exciting to have a challenge or a cause in life, to live for a cause, no matter what it is. It doesn't give me great pleasure when I do things for myself. I'll be very happy if I give from myself to people around me. It doesn't matter whether they're my people or not. For example, look now, I am teaching here in Canada, and the only thing that is in common between me and the kids or the parents is we are human beings. That's all.

I didn't want to leave. Until the very last moment, I didn't want to leave, but after thirteen years you get tired. I was giving, giving, giving, not getting anything. I felt that if I'm going to stay there, something wrong was going to happen to me.

Well, when I came here, I was not equipped. It was like being a soldier going to a big battle — no weapons, nothing — just myself and my belief in myself and God. That's all that I brought with me. Everything was so discouraging. I didn't go to school here, my English was not very good. I didn't have confidence, I was tired, I didn't know whether I was going to make it or not. I didn't have money, and I didn't want my family to help me, though they did. I was living with my cousins in a small apartment. They were happy! And I was very happy the first six months. I'd rest and I gained weight, six kilos. I wondered why do people get depressed here? Why are they upset? When we go on the bus or when we go shopping if people have a serious face or they're not smiling I ask why. There's no reason to be so serious or worried; they have no reason at all. It's peaceful, they can go everywhere they want. The government is like a family to everybody.

I never thought that they were going to reject my cousin's sponsorship of me at Immigration. I thought it was nice to spend one year here and then go back. I decided to take courses here, like English as a second language, then I'd go back to Lebanon. I'd take new experiences, new things with me, which is nice. After one year, I was sure I'd be much better than when I left, but that was not the case because they rejected my application. They wanted me to go back to Lebanon and to apply from there. So that's why I had to become a refugee — because that was the only way to stay in the country. At that time, it was very bad, the situation in Lebanon, and I couldn't go back anyway, so I stayed, and it took them a long time to give me a work permit. It was very boring, very frustrating. I took a course at a college, and I took another course here and there, but that was not what I wanted. I was taking the courses just to feel that I'm doing something, like anybody here. I know the first year, I was very, very miserable and upset and depressed. I found it very, very hard, after suffering thirteen years in Lebanon, to come to Canada and claim refugee.

It was something burning, as if I had all the mountains around here, Vancouver, on my shoulders. It was very hard because I was in the air, I was not on a solid base. In Lebanon I was upset, I was depressed and everything, but I was on a solid base, with a family, the land. But here I was like a feather in the air, the wind. You don't know where you are going to be. You are nothing here, nothing at all. You have to start from the very beginning. It took me a while to stand up on my feet. I was not working, and it was not because I can't work, or I don't want to work, it was because I am a refugee. So after suffering thirteen years, I came here to stand at the doors of Immigration, claiming refugee.

The second year, my mom got sick. She wanted me to go back and I couldn't leave the country. They didn't tell me it was serious, that it was cancer — they didn't say that — and after that she died. I couldn't go back to see. It was the worst part of my life. We struggled so hard, me and her, and we survived. And the moment I turned my back, she was sick. It was very sad, very frustrating. It took me more than two years — until I went back last summer, actually — to believe that. That was the time I started to ask is it worth it? — to leave everything behind and come here because I never thought that something like that would happen in our family.

# LYN

You were telling me about a girlfriend of yours who told you about how hard it would be here in Canada. Did you go back and talk to her?

# MIRA

She couldn't believe it. She thought that I changed. After four years, I thought that she was going to be more flexible and more mature, and I found that she was still in the same place. But she found that I had changed. I'm stronger, I am more flexible and I have courage.

When any immigrant, whether a man or woman, loses somebody in the family, it hurts a lot. You start to think why am I here? Is it worth it? Wasn't it much nicer and better to be beside them? They need me. So this was the worst part. It took me a long time to recover. Mother to me now is not my biological mother. It's the land, the country, when I talk about mother or motherhood. These are things we start to think about or feel when we are far away. So now my mother died, but I still belong, very strongly, somewhere — to the land. I envy people who have the chance to stay wherever they live their childhood and they put their first roots.

This is one of the things that's very hard. You get to learn a lot, it's very, very nice to be far away, to learn about different people, different cultures, to be free, to be important and everything, but it doesn't help you. As an immigrant, it doesn't help you. It doesn't change anything because where you're established or where you started your first roots it's very important.

My composure was shattered as Mira spoke about her tragic circumstances and her flight from Lebanon. My life in Vancouver was relatively comfortable, orderly and peaceful, far from the upheavals that still rack Lebanon and the Arab world. Mira's story was so vast, so complex, so full of life and feeling, that all the theory I had been studying seemed inadequate in comparison. Her story is a testimonial to the resilience of the human spirit, a tribute to a woman who has maintained a lifelong commitment to personal growth despite the traumas of civil war and migration. Mira has faced social change throughout her life, for the very fabric of Lebanese society and culture has changed dramatically over the last century, changes accelerated by modernisation and war. Though Mira was raised in a small mountain village, she grew up to become a middle-class professional, critical of certain aspects and some sectors of her society. When she immigrated to Canada she was moving between complex modern societies in which she could continue her commitment to her profession and to her values.

During four months of interviews, our roles of narrator and investigator took on new dimensions. With Mira's stories and interpretations dominating our sessions, I came to feel more like a student, with Mira as my teacher. When we attended a few Lebanese community events together I found myself relying upon Mira to explain traditional customs and behaviour patiently. The direction of my research was shaped by the themes that she thought most important, like culture shock.

## MIRA

For any immigrant this is the main topic: culture shock. Whether you are aware of it or not, it's there. But it depends on how you express it, how you talk about it, how you live it, how you deal with it.

## LYN

What was it for you?

## MIRA

It was shocking! As you know, it was not my first visit to Canada or to North America. It was my third visit. The first time I stayed in Canada was 1980. I stayed only for five months, so I had an idea of what life is. It's not as if I was not ready, but there were many things that I had no clue about before I came here. I remember a few things that we used to discuss and talk about, me and my friends in Lebanon, when they knew that I was leaving for Canada. They said "Mira, are you aware, are you ready? There are so many things that are totally different. You are a girl, it's not like a guy." They have more freedom, the man in the Middle East. Whether they are in Lebanon or outside Lebanon, they want to live on their own, they want to travel, it's no problem, but when it comes to the women, or the girls, we have to think twice about taking decisions because it's not easy.

When I was in Lebanon it was not that difficult there. If I wanted a job, I didn't have to apply because the school knows my father or my brothers. It's below my dignity to go and *apply* for a job. Now when I came to Canada and I started to look for a job — staying here for two years without working it was something very, very, very difficult for me.

Something else, the family life here, it was really shocking. For example, to have single mothers. We don't have this. If you have children in Lebanon this means you are married. It was a big shock to me when one time I met a lady with her son, who was maybe two years old. So we're talking and I asked her something about her husband, and she said, "I'm not married." I said, "Oh. So where did you get this boy?"

## LYN

What were you thinking when you said that?

## MIRA

Not married? You have a child and not married? This is a shock. I'd heard about single mothers and everything, so I didn't say anything. In Lebanon, for example, or in the Middle East, if you ask a child about his father, and he says his father is dead, you know people feel so sorry for him. I felt so sorry for the children and sorry for the woman herself because it's very sad. Children need father and mother. When I think about myself — how important my dad and my mother are in my life, maybe because of the way I was brought up, maybe because my mom and my dad were so close and they had good relations and it was reflected on us, so I couldn't imagine it. I thought that everybody else is the same. And the rate of divorce is very low in Lebanon. Now I understand why it's like that. It took a long time, but I couldn't understand before.

This would never happen in Lebanon. It is out of the question. This is one of the advantages of being so close, living in a society which is family-oriented. There is something that we have to remember, that I lived with my cousin when I came, so had I had to live on my own, it would be a totally different story. I still had the feeling at that time that I'm living at home. People can understand you, you don't have to translate or explain.

Something else. It was not shocking, but it was surprising: when people talk about animals here. They love animals, they respect animals, they care a lot for animals and pets, especially for pets. I sent a letter home and I told them how nice it is here and how lucky people are here and how lucky the cats are here and the dogs.

Now I've got used to how people think, I know why they do that. There were so many things that I couldn't understand because I didn't know what they mean or why they do that. I didn't know that the cat or the dog is very important in the life of a lonely person here. I didn't know that people were so lonely and they need anything, even an animal. Really, it's very sad. I understand that, definitely, and it's a very important thing, thank God that there are animals and pets like this.

## LYN

Do you think people ever become lonely like that in Lebanon?

## MIRA

No way. In Lebanon you have to find a way to be by yourself for a few minutes.

## LYN

Was that a surprise for you, to discover that people could be lonely?

## MIRA

It was very sad. I felt so sad, and now, sometimes, we are lonely here. I mean, we have friends and everything, but we still feel that we are lonely because we know how our families are living there, our friends are living there, so this is not enough for us. We come from work, you cook dinner, you eat and that's it. On the weekend you socialise, or you see people, or you go somewhere and that's it. Even though you go with friends, you still feel that something big is missing.

## LYN

Do you think that your feeling about life has changed at all since you've come here?

# MIRA

I've become more aware of things and more practical and more flexible and more experienced. Practical means, for example, if something didn't work out, it's not the end of the world, we can do something else, if not exactly, something similar. A little less, a little more, it doesn't matter. Before I would say "No! It has to be like that." As I told you, I was over-protected in Lebanon. I didn't have the chance to see because I had this big umbrella, a beautiful parasol. It was very nice, but I couldn't see anything beyond it. So now, once the beautiful umbrella was removed, I was able to use my own eyes and see the sky and the clouds and the rain and the rainbow and everything by my own eye.

After living three years in Canada, Mira was no longer shocked by Canadian family life. But as she spoke, I realised that didn't mean that she unquestioningly accepted Canadian ways. Instead, she found a way to understand and explain them, based on her own expanding frame of reference. Culture shock provided the catalyst for Mira's learning. Culture shock used to be considered a kind of mental illness, but now it's believed to be the core of cross-cultural learning, a stress that triggers learning to adapt and change.

With each shock, Mira reflected on her assumptions, becoming aware of alternatives to the "beautiful umbrella" of her previous ideas. Mira realised that there were different ways of seeing the world, that she could see by her own eyes. She didn't have to unlearn or forget to change her perspective, though she did learn about new feelings, like loneliness, that shape human relationships. She developed a more critical awareness of herself and of what she shared with other Lebanese, the things that provided structure and meaning to Lebanese society. With this new found awareness, Mira could make comparisons and judgements about Canadians and Lebanese ways. She had the opportunity to see "the rainbow," to cope with life in Canada with new understanding, flexibility and practicality. She could see negative aspects as well, "clouds," like selfishness and loneliness.

When I first met Mira, I thought that she had been successful in adapting, in conforming to Canadian norms, but as I talked with her, I realised that she had quietly resisted both social and cultural domination by minimizing her participation in Canadian society. Though she resented being forced to claim refugee status, she had learned that there can be advantages to being a peripheral participant in a community. After her immigration, Mira adapted by accepting and acting on some of the assumptions of Canadian society while resisting others. She felt more confident as she discovered cultural meanings that were shared among Canadians and shaped her own interpretations of them. As she revised her understanding, Mira constructed her own interpretation of culture.

Mira saw no contradiction in her cultural identity. She was living in Canada, not becoming Canadian. She was participating in Canadian society but maintaining her links to Lebanon by phone, letters and occasional visits. Instead of having two selves, Mira had two homes.

Having listened to Mira's story, I have begun to reinterpret identity. I now see it as a complex, dynamic web of perspectives, commitments and dimensions. Mira has revised her identity through "flexibility and practicality" — her changing perspectives and sense of agency. As Mira reflected, worked out strategies and made decisions, she constructed her own identity and decided on her actions from a broadening repertoire of possibilities. Amidst the discontinuities of her life in Canada, her ethnic identity provided a sense of continuity and stability, even as she began to articulate and reflect upon herself in a pluralistic society and culture. Her Lebanese identity strengthened her autonomy and her ability to accept or resist aspects of Canadian culture.

As I learned more about Lebanese and Canadian families from Mira, it dawned on me that I was learning about being Lebanese through her stories, just as she had learned about being Canadian through sharing stories with Canadian women. Her life in Canada had, in a way, become her research project, motivated by her refugee status and her search for an alternative home and by her lifelong commitment to personal growth.

From an unpublished study,
*"Seeing Things From Different Corners: A Story of Learning and Culture."*

# REFERENCES

Caffarella, R.S., and Olson, S.K. *Psychosocial Development of Women: A Critical Review of the Literature* in **Adult Education Quarterly**, Vol. 43, No. 3, 1993, pp. 125-151.

Gilligan, C. *In a Different Voice: Psychological Theory and Women's Development* (Cambridge, Massachusetts: Harvard University Press, 1982).

Eickelman, D. *The Middle East: An Anthropological Approach* (Englewood Cliffs, New Jersey: Prentice Hall, 1989).

Keddie, N., and Beck, L. Introduction to *Women in the Muslim World*. Beck, L. and Keddie, N., eds. (Cambridge, Massachusetts:Harvard University Press, 1978), pp. 1-34.

Nelson, C. *Public and Private Politics: Women in the Middle Eastern World"* in **The American Ethnologist**, Vol. 1, No. 3, 1974,pp. 551-563.

### Jasmine Dodd
# Going Home

I planned and saved. Anticipation had my stomach in knots
I smiled when I saw jealousy on my friend's faces —
barely visible under scarves, wincing in the cold —

I was going home.

Home, where I could walk the streets
And nod and smile and greet my extended family with their due "mornin"

Home, beside and between and among them all
No defending or challenging or shrinking or labelling here

Home. Warmth. Relief.
Customs.

ADMITTED TO THE ISLAND AS VISITOR. MAXIMUM STAY 15
DAYS.  MAY NOT ACCEPT GAINFUL EMPLOYMENT.

"Welcome Home."

I smiled.

# BIOGRAPHIES

## Joanne Arnott

Joanne Arnott is the author of two books of poetry, Wiles of Girlhood and My Grass Cradle, and one children's book, Ma MacDonald. Wiles of Girlhood won the Canadian League of Poet's Gerald Lampert Award for best first book of poetry. Joanne is a Métis writer, the mother of three and the facilitator for Unlearning Racism and Political Context of Mothering workshops. Breasting the Waves is the title of her forthcoming collection of nonfiction writings.

## Anurita Bains

Anurita Bains is a freelance writer whose work has appeared in This Magazine, Now Magazine, The Toronto Star and the Sikh Press.

## Louise Bak

Louise Bak is a third generation Chinese-Canadian writer, born in Kingston, Ontario. She is working on an M.A. in East Asian women's history. Louise lives in downtown Toronto where she is happy when horseradish sneaks up on her in the night.

# Ayanna Black

Born in Jamaica, Ayanna Black lived in England before coming to Canada in 1964. Her books include No Contingencies and two anthologies, Voices: Canadian Writers of African Descent and Fiery Spirits.

# Josee Brome

Josee Brome was born in 1963 in Montreal to Bajan parents and is "still trying to find my place."

# Joyce Brown

Joyce Brown is a sixth generation African-Canadian. She has an Honours English degree from McMaster University, is a poet and playwright, an actress with Sojourner's Truth Theatre Company and a Black feminist activist.

# Dawn Carter

Dawn Carter is a British-born, Alberta-raised, Afro-Canadian writer, primarily of poetry and short stories. She has given several readings in the Edmonton area and was published in the1993 and 1994 Stroll of Poets Anthologies.

# Alison Chan

Alison Chan was born in Hong Kong and attends Queen's University. Her interests include music, anthropology, history and cooking. Her musical skills range from playing the piano and the viola to playing the bagpipes.

# Caroline Chan

Caroline Chan was born in Hong Kong, which she last visited in the summer of 1995. She spent a year working there in 1988. She received a Bachelor of Fine Arts from the Nova Scotia College of Art and Design in 1992. She is a visual artist and arts administrator and lives in Halifax. Her work has been exhibited in Halifax and Toronto.

# Geoffrey Chan

Geoffrey Chan was born in Hong Kong and is finishing his undergraduate studies at Trent University in the Environmental and the Cultural Studies programs. He took a year off studying to return to Hong Kong in 1994 to dig up old haunts and to travel. While there, he worked for the World Wildlife Fund at Mai Po Marshes.

# Jennifer Chan

Jennifer Chan was born in Toronto. She is a pensive ninth grader who enjoys sports, writing, horseback riding and following the Toronto Blue Jays.

# Jaya Chauhan and Melody Sylvestre

Jaya Chauhan and Melody Sylvestre first met in 1990 in Antigonish, Nova Scotia, where they both lived. Jaya now lives in Edmonton and Melody in Toronto. Jaya works for the Dreamspeakers Festival Society and Melody works for the Community Services Department of the Social Services Division of the Municipality of Metropolitan Toronto.

# Annette Clough

Annette Clough is a Gemini snake who lives in Toronto with her dear life partner and their wonderful daughter. If she ever gets out of women's services, she would like to be a photographer.

# Mutriba Din

Mutriba Din describes herself as "a feminist who agrees wholeheartedly with Toni Cade Bambara that the work is "to make revolution irresistible."

# Jasmine Dodd

Jasmine Dodd was born in Canada, grew up in Jamaica and now lives in Toronto.

# Lorena Gale

Born in Montreal, Lorena Gale, is a third-plus-generation Canadian of African, First Nations and South Asian descent. An actor, director, writer and a mother, Lorena is a former artistic director of the Black Theatre Workshop in Montreal and the creator and coordinator of a program for the professional development of artists of colour in the theatre. She lives in Vancouver.

# Camille Hernandez-Ramdwar

Camille Hernandez-Ramdwar is a "TrinCan" living in Toronto. She is research-ing the construction of race in Canada and the Caribbean as it relates to people of mixed heritage.

# Lynette Harper and Mira

Lynette Harper and Mira live in Nanaimo, British Columbia.

# Silvana Hernando

Silvano Hernando is a Latino lesbian who hopes to move back home to Argentina with her partner. Meanwhile, she keeps her roots alive by doing *mate* with her friends.

# Camille Isaacs

Camille Isaacs, of Guyanese parentage, was born and raised in Toronto. She has a B.A. in English from the University of Toronto and completed an M.A. in English at the University of the West Indies in Jamaica. She works as a freelance editor. "Most of my life I have felt the pull between a "Canadian" lifestyle and a "West Indian" one. I believe part of the solution lies in widening the definition of what it means to be Canadian, so that people of colour no longer need to be asked "... but where are you really from?"

# Susan Lee

A recent graduate from the University of Western Ontario, Susan Lee now lives in Toronto.

# Nadine Leggett

Nadine Leggett was raised in southern Ontario. Adopted as an infant by White parents, she grew up in a racially-mixed family. She studied psychology and sociology at York University and later trained as an art therapist.

# Brenda Joy Lem

Brenda Joy Lem is a writer, artist, filmmaker and community activist.

# Barbara Malanka

Barbara Malanka's writing has appeared in periodicals and in the anthology, Miscegenation Blues: Voices of Mixed Race Women. A political activist, she is engaged in the movement against violence against women and is the president of the Ontario Coalition of Rape Crisis Centres. She enjoys chance encounters with moose north of the Arctic Watershed, slow dancing in the wee hours, collecting coins from around the world, classic films of the 1940s and 50s, swing, jazz, Strauss waltzes, soaring over Georgian Bay at 20,000 feet and hosting potluck parties for her friends. She is working on her first novel a lesbian thriller and on the outline for a video documentary about women of colour who work within the predominately White middle-class women's movement.

# Janice McCurdy Banigan

Janice McCurdy Banigan was born in Windsor, Ontario, has four children and four grandchildren, writes on social activism, health and multiculturalism, is a playwright and has had her play "Free T' Be!" produced and workshopped twice by Theatre Passe Muraille in Toronto. She has written two other books, A Sense of Mission, about her years as the director of the Downtown Mission, a crisis intervention and drop-in centre, and Like the Leaves, a child's multi-cultural story book. She is working on her third book.

## Hazelle Palmer

Hazelle Palmer is a journalist, author and painter. Her first book, *Tales from the Gardens and Beyond* is a collection of vignettes that capture the lives of the women who settle in a working class neighbourhood in 1960s Montreal. Her articles have appeared in Canadian Women Studies/les cahier de la femme, Fuse Magazine, diva, Healthsharing Magazine, Books In Canada, Revue Noire, and the Toronto Star. Born in London, England and raised in Montreal, Palmer now lives in Toronto with her partner Alfred and their daughter Ashae.

## Althea Samuels

Althea Samuels is a writer living in Ottawa. Her work has appeared in The Ottawa Citizen, the Ottawa-Carleton Teachers' Workbook on Ethnocultural and Race Relations and Sharing our Experience, a publication of the Canadian Advisory Council on the Status of Women. She has worked with the Jamaican, Barbadian and Guyanese associations in Ottawa and volunteers as a class parent at her daughter's school.

## Michelle P. Scott

Michelle P. Scott was born and raised in Toronto. Writing has always been one of her pleasurable pastimes. A graduate of the University of Toronto with aspirations of a career in medicine, she lives in Toronto.

## Karen Shadd-Evelyn

Karen Shadd-Evelyn is a sixth-generation Black Canadian from North Buxton, Ontario. Her poetry, short stories and articles have appeared in various publications. Her book, I'd Rather Live in Buxton, chronicles growing up in that small

Black Canadian community. "Mother Africa: A Drum Song for Scattered Harvests," won first prize in the Canadian League of Black Artists Inc. first National Black Poetry competition in 1995.

## Carol Talbot

Born in Windsor, Ontario, Carol Talbot teaches English in London, Ontario. Her published works include Growing Up Black in Canada, which won her an Excellence in Education certificate and pin from the Ontario Secondary Teacher's Federation in London. Her poetry appears in Canada in Us Now and Other Voices and in other anthologies. Carol received a new playwright's award from Theatre Fountainhead for "The Gathering."

## Lisa Valencia-Svensson

Lisa Valencia-Svensson describes herself as "a half-breed Filipina-Canadian dyke" who feels "there is no place that people of colour will ever find in this society. We will have to fight for every bit of space we make for ourselves here."